ECONOMIC ISSUES, PROBLEMS AND PERSPECTIVES

FEDERAL TAXATION

Economic Issues, Problems and Perspectives

Additional books in this series can be found on Nova's website under the Series tab.

Additional E-books in this series can be found on Nova's website under the E-book tab.

Congressional Policies, Practices and Procedures

Additional books in this series can be found on Nova's website under the Series tab.

Additional E-books in this series can be found on Nova's website under the E-book tab.

ECONOMIC ISSUES, PROBLEMS AND PERSPECTIVES

FEDERAL TAXATION

JACLYN N. PRICHARD
EDITOR

Nova Science Publishers, Inc.
New York

For permission to use material from this book please contact us:
Telephone 631-231-7269; Fax 631-231-8175
Web Site: http://www.novapublishers.com

Library of Congress Cataloging-in-Publication Data

Federal taxation / editor, Jaclyn N. Prichard.
p. cm.
Includes index.
ISBN 978-1-61324-102-8 (hardcover)
1. Taxation--United States. I. Prichard, Jaclyn N.
HJ2362.F43 2011
336.200973--dc22 2011008465

Published by Nova Science Publishers, Inc. † New York

CONTENTS

PREFACE

The President and leading members of Congress have stated that fundamental tax reform is a major policy objective for the 112th Congress. These policymakers have said that fundamental tax reform is needed in order to raise a large amount of additional revenue, which is necessary to reduce high forecast budget deficits and the sharply rising national debt. Congressional interest has been expressed in both a major overhaul of the U.S. tax system and the feasibility of levying a consumption tax. This new book examines the federal tax structure, provides some statistics on the tax system as a whole, tax reform, and presents analysis of selected tax concepts.

Chapter 1- The major sources of federal tax revenue are individual income taxes, Social Security and other payroll taxes, corporate income taxes, excise taxes, and estate and gift taxes. This report describes the federal tax structure, provides some statistics on the tax system as a whole, and presents analysis of selected tax concepts.

Chapter 2- Congressional interest has been expressed in both a major overhaul of the U.S. tax system and the feasibility of levying a consumption tax. Some proponents of reform argue that the tax base should be broadened by reducing or eliminating many tax expenditures. Tax expenditures are revenue losses resulting from federal tax provisions that grant special tax relief designed to encourage certain kinds of behavior by taxpayers or to aid taxpayers in special circumstances. If tax expenditures are reduced substantially or a consumption tax is levied or both, then the marginal income tax rates could be reduced. An alternative to increasing tax revenues is cutting spending. Thus, members are faced with considering the best mix of tax increases and spending cuts in order to reduce deficits and slow the growth of the national debt.

Chapter 3- A foundation of the broad tax revisions implemented 24 years ago by the Tax Reform Act of 1986 was tax "neutrality"—the idea that economic efficiency and economic welfare are promoted if the distorting impact of taxes on business and other economic decisions is minimized. Based on this principle, the 1986 act broadened the tax base and reduced statutory tax rates set forth by the tax code. In time, however, the underlying thrust of tax policy has changed. Rather than neutrality and efficiency, recent business tax legislation has been guided more by a concern for promoting investment and capital formation, and by attention to the perceived impact of taxes on the ability of U.S. firms to compete with foreign companies. Further, recent interest in fundamental tax reform has been partly stimulated by these same concerns for capital formation and competitiveness.

Chapter 4- At the end of 2010, the lower income tax rates provided in 2001 were to expire. The President had proposed to extend most tax cuts, but to continue higher rates for couples with income over $250,000 and singles with income over $200,000. The most important element of this proposal, as measured by revenue effect, is allowing the top rates of 33% and 35% to expire, when they would have risen to 36% and 36.9%. P.L. 111-312, enacted in December 2010, extended all tax cuts for two years, through 2012, delaying the consideration of which tax cuts to retain.

Chapter 5- One provision of the 1913 individual income tax that generated a great deal of confusion was the taxation of income from the sale of property (i.e., capital gains income). This initial confusion has led to almost 100 years of legislative debates over capital gains. Beginning in 1922, capital gains were first subject to lower tax rates than ordinary income. This preferential treatment has continued throughout most of the history of the income tax. Proposals dealing with the taxation of capital gains have ranged from the outright elimination of capital gains taxation to the reduction of capital gains tax rates for certain classes of taxpayers to the elimination of the preferential tax treatment.

Chapter 6- Tax legislation in 1997 reduced capital gains taxes on several types of assets, imposing a 20% maximum tax rate on long-term gains, a rate temporarily reduced to 15% for 2003-2008, which was extended for two additional years in 2006. Legislation enacted in December 2010 extended the lower rates for an additional two years, thorough 2010.There is also an exclusion of $500,000 ($250,000 for single returns) for gains on home sales. The capital gains tax has been a tax cut target since the 1986 Tax Reform Act treated capital gains as ordinary income. An argument for lower capital gains taxes is reduction of the lock-in effect. Some also believe that lower capital gains taxes will cost little compared to the benefits they bring and that lower taxes induce additional economic growth, although the magnitude of these potential effects is in some dispute. Others criticize lower capital gains taxes as benefitting higher income individuals and express concerns about the budget effects, particularly in future years. Another criticism of lower rates is the possible role of a larger capital gains tax differential in encouraging tax sheltering activities and adding complexity to the tax law.

Chapter 7 According to the Social Security Trustees, assets in the two Social Security trust funds will be exhausted by 2037, and, thereafter, Social Security payroll tax revenues will cover about three-quarters of promised benefits. Over the past decade several proposals have been put forward which could help to close the Social Security program's long-term financing gap. One proposal would increase the Social Security payroll tax base so that 90% of covered earnings are taxable— the same proportion as in 1982. This policy would increase the payroll taxes paid by higher-earning workers and not affect workers earning less than the current Social Security maximum taxable limit, which is $106,800 in 2010.

Chapter 8- American drivers, compared to those in other industrialized nations in Europe, pay relatively low federal, state, and local gasoline and diesel excise taxes. The federal taxes are used specifically to fund annual highway construction, maintenance, and mass transit. Over the years, proposals have come forth to raise the federal tax as a way to address long-standing national policy concerns, including U.S. dependence on imported oil and various environmental problems related to large volumes of gasoline consumption.

In: Federal Taxation
Editor: Jaclyn N. Prichard

ISBN: 978-1-61324-102-8

Chapter 1

OVERVIEW OF THE FEDERAL TAX SYSTEM*

Molly F. Sherlock and Donald J. Marples

SUMMARY

The major sources of federal tax revenue are individual income taxes, Social Security and other payroll taxes, corporate income taxes, excise taxes, and estate and gift taxes. This report describes the federal tax structure, provides some statistics on the tax system as a whole, and presents analysis of selected tax concepts.

The federal income tax is levied on an individual's taxable income, which is adjusted gross income (AGI) less deduction and exemptions. Tax rates, based on filing status (e.g., married filing jointly or single individual) determine the level of tax liability. Tax rates in the United States are progressive, such that higher levels of income are taxed at higher rates. Once tax liability is calculated, tax credits can be used to reduce tax liability. Tax deductions and tax credits are tools available to policymakers to increase or decrease the after-tax price of undertaking specific activities. Individuals with high levels of exemptions, deductions, and credits relative to income may be required to file under the alternative minimum tax (AMT).

Corporate taxable income is also subject to varying rates, where those with higher levels of income pay higher levels of taxes. Social Security and Medicare tax rates are, respectively, 12.4% and 2.9%. In 2010, Social Security taxes are levied on the first $106,800 of wages, with the wage cap

---

* This is an edited, reformatted and augmented version of Congressional Research Services publication RL32808, dated September 16, 2010.

adjusted annually for increases in average wages in the economy. Medicare taxes are assessed against all wage income. Federal excise taxes are levied on specific goods, such as transportation fuels, alcohol, tobacco, and telephones.

In FY2009, individual income taxes accounted for 44% of total federal revenue. Social Security taxes accounted for 42%. Corporate income taxes accounted for 7% while excise taxes accounted for 3%. Estate and gift, customs, and miscellaneous taxes accounted for the remaining 5% of total revenue. Over time, corporate income tax has become much less important as a revenue source while Social Security taxes have provided a larger share of total revenues.

Analysis of tax statistics from the federal tax system as a whole leads to three conclusions: (1) federal revenue as a percentage of GDP is in line with historical trends; (2) the U.S. fiscal position is in line with the fiscal position of other industrialized nations (revenues and expenditures as a percentage of GDP are relatively low); and (3) over the past decade, effective tax rates have fallen for individuals at all income levels, but have fallen more for lower-income individuals, reducing their share of overall tax liabilities.

The final sections of this report analyze a number of tax concepts. Tax expenditures are revenue losses from special tax deductions, credits, and other benefits. Capital gains warrant special attention, as there is debate about their being taxed at a lower rate. Marriage tax penalties and bonuses, while reduced following legislation enacted in 2001 and 2003, still pose an inequity in the tax system. Tax deferral, or the timing of taxes, poses problems related to the timing of taxation, specifically with respect to capital gains. Depreciation is important, as accelerated depreciation schemes or expensing can influence firm behavior. Tax liability also depends on form of business organization. Finally, the issue of whether taxes can influence firms' competitiveness is reviewed.

This report will be updated on enactment of major changes in the federal tax system.

INTRODUCTION

The major sources of federal tax revenue are individual income taxes, Social Security and other payroll taxes, corporate income taxes, excise taxes, and estate and gift taxes. This report describes the federal tax structure, provides some statistics on the tax system as a whole, and presents analysis of selected tax concepts.

FEDERAL TAXES: A DESCRIPTION

The individual income tax is the major source of federal revenues, followed closely by Social Security and other payroll taxes. As a revenue source, the corporate income tax is a distant third. Estate and gift and excise taxes play only minor roles as revenue sources.

The Structure of the Federal Individual Income Tax

The individual income tax is based on earnings individuals accrue from a variety of sources. Included in the individual income tax base are wages, salaries, tips, taxable interest and dividend income, business and farm income, realized net capital gains, income from rents, royalties, trusts, estates, partnerships, taxable pension and annuity income, and alimony received.

The tax base is reduced by adjustments to income, including contributions to Keogh and traditional IRAs, some interest paid on student loans and higher education expenses, contributions to health savings accounts, and alimony payments made by the taxpayer. This step of the process produces adjusted gross income (AGI), which is the basic measure of income under the federal income tax. Deductions from the income tax base that result in an individual's AGI are also known as "above the line" deductions. These deductions are available to all taxpayers, whether the taxpayer chooses to take the standard deduction or itemize deductions.[1]

The tax base is further reduced by either the standard deduction or individuals' itemized deductions.[2] Itemized deductions are allowed for home mortgage interest payments, state and local income taxes, state and local property taxes, charitable contributions, medical expenses in excess of 7.5% of AGI, and for a variety of other items. For taxable years 2004 through 2009, at the election of the taxpayer, state and local sales taxes can be deducted as an alternative to state and local income taxes.[3] Proposals have been made to extend the sales tax deduction option through 2010. An extension of the sales tax deduction option was approved by the House on December 9, 2009, as part of the Tax Extenders Act of 2009 (H.R. 4213). The American Jobs and Closing Loopholes Act of 2010 (a revised version of H.R. 4213) also contains provisions that would extend this sales tax deduction option.

The tax base is reduced further by subtracting personal and dependent exemptions. Exemptions are a fixed amount to be subtracted from AGI. Exemptions are allowed for the taxpayer, the taxpayer's spouse, and each dependent. In 2010, the exemption amount per person is $3,650.[4] For taxpayers with high levels of AGI, the personal and dependent exemptions are phased out.[5]

Federal income taxes are assessed on a taxpayer's taxable income. Taxable income equals AGI reduced by either the standard deductions or itemized deductions and personal and dependent exemptions. **Figure 1** illustrates the computation of taxable income.

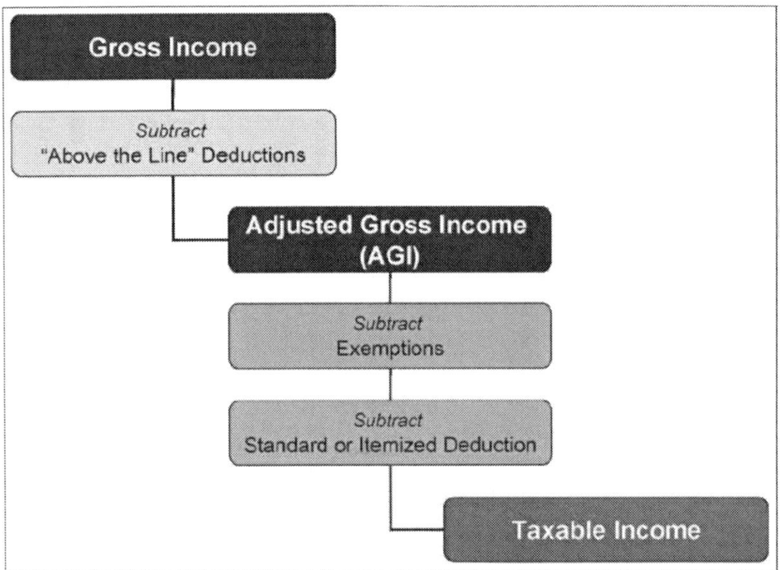

Source: CRS.

Figure 1. Computing Taxable Income.

The tax liability depends on the filing status of the taxpayer. There are four main filing categories: married filing jointly, married filing separately, head of household, and single individual. The computation of a taxpayer's tax liability depends on their filing status.

The income tax system is designed to be progressive, with marginal tax rates increasing as income increases.[6] At a particular marginal tax rate, all individuals, regardless of their level of earnings, pay the same tax rate on their first dollar of taxable income. Once a taxpayer's income surpasses a threshold level placing them in a higher marginal tax bracket, the higher marginal tax rate is only applied on income that exceeds that threshold value. Currently, the individual income tax system has six marginal income tax rates: 10%, 15%, 25%, 28%, 33%, and 35%.[7]

These marginal income tax rates are applied against taxable income to arrive at a taxpayer's gross income tax liability.

After a taxpayer's tax liability has been calculated, tax credits are subtracted from gross tax liability to arrive at a final tax liability. Major tax credits include the earned income tax credit, the child tax credit, education tax credits, and the credit for child and dependent care expenses.

Not all income is subject to the marginal income tax rates noted above. Long-term capital gains— that is, gain on the sale of assets held more than 12 months— and qualified dividend income are taxed at lower tax rates.[8]

Gross Income and Adjustments

In order to levy an income tax, income must first be defined. As a benchmark, economists often turn to the Haig-Simons comprehensive income definitions. Here, taxable resources are defined as changes in a taxpayer's ability to consume during the tax year.[9] Another way to view the individual income tax base is as an approximation of the sum of all labor and capital income earned or received over the course of the year. Under this view, the tax base resembles national income as measured by economists. In addition to labor and capital income, many transfer payments are also subject to taxation.

There are a number of forms of what would broadly be defined as income that are excluded from taxable income in practice. For example, wage income of employees is taxed, although most contributions to employee pension and health insurance plans and certain other employee benefits are not included in wages subject to income tax. Employer contributions to Social Security are also excluded from wages. When pensions are received, they are included in income to the extent that they represent contributions originally excluded. If the taxpayer has the same tax rate when contributions are made and when pensions are received, this treatment is equivalent to eliminating tax on the earnings of pension plans. Some Social Security benefits are also subject to tax.

Passive capital income, in the form of capital gains, interest, and dividends on financial instruments, is also taxed. The tax base excludes capital gains that are unrealized, such that capital gains are only taxed on realization. The current tax rate on realized capital gains is 15%.[10] Unlike capital gains, assets earning interest are taxed on accrual. Taxes are paid on the interest earned in each tax year.[11] Taxable interest income is added to a taxpayer's AGI and taxed according to the taxpayer's marginal tax rate. Interest that is earned on tax-exempt securities, such as those issued by state and local governments, is not subject to taxation. Like capital gains, dividends are taxed at a lower rate than other income. Qualified dividends are taxed at the same rate as capital gains.[12] Absent legislative action, dividends income will be subject to ordinary tax rates beginning in 2011.[13]

Income from operating a business through a proprietorship, partnership, or small business corporation that elects to be treated similarly to a partnership (Subchapter S corporation), or through rental property (which reflects returns to both investment and effort) is also subject to tax, although it is always difficult to measure such income precisely.[14] This income is the net of gross receipts reduced by such deductible costs as payments to labor, depreciation, costs of goods acquired for resale and other inputs, interest, and taxes. Some investment income of small businesses is subject to favorable treatment through provisions that allow costs of capital equipment to be expensed. Other income, such as miscellaneous income, gambling winnings, and royalties, is also included in the tax base.

As noted above, there are several adjustments to the income made to determine adjusted gross income (AGI). These are the so-called "above the line" deductions noted above. As was illustrated in Figure 1, deductions and exemptions are subtracted from AGI to determine taxable income. The next section provides more detail on these deductions and exemptions.

Deductions and Exemptions

Individuals subtract from their adjusted gross income either the standard deduction or itemized deductions, along with an exemption for each family member. The standard deduction and personal exemption are indexed for inflation. The most common deductions for taxpayers choosing to itemize were listed above. Personal exemptions and standard deductions from 2004 through 2010 are given in Table 1.

Table 1. Statutory Personal Exemptions and Standard Deductions

Filing Status	2004	2005	2006	2007	2008	2009	2010
Personal Exemptions	$3,100	$3,200	$3,300	$3,400	$3,500	$3,650	$3,650
Standard Deductions							
—Married Filing Jointly	$9,700	$10,000	$10,300	$10,700	$10,900	$11,400	$11,400
—Single Individual	$4,850	$5,000	$5,150	$5,350	$5,450	$5,700	$5,700
—Head of Household	$7,150	$7,300	$7,750	$7,850	$8,000	$8,350	$8,400

Source: Internal Revenue Code.

Notes: For married couples filing separately the personal exemption and standard deduction is half of that allowed for married couples filing jointly.

Historically, personal exemptions and itemized deductions have been limited for certain high-income taxpayers.[15] Provisions under the Economic Growth and Tax Relief Reconciliation Act of 2001 (EGTRRA; P.L. 107-16) gradually reduced the personal exemption phaseout (PEP), such that the phaseout was completely repealed in 2010. President Obama's FY2011 Budget Proposal, if enacted, would reinstate the personal exemption phaseout for high income taxpayers.

Before 2010, itemized deductions were limited above a certain threshold.[16] Like PEP, the limitation on itemized deductions, also known as Pease, was phased out under EGTRRA. By 2010, the Pease limitation was repealed. The Pease-related provisions of EGTRRA are scheduled to expire at the end of 2010. President Obama's FY2011 Budget proposes to reinstate the Pease limitations for married couples filing jointly with an AGI of more than $250,000 and single filers with an AGI of more than $200,000. For the 2009 PEP and Pease phaseout limits, see the Appendix.

Tax Rates

Tax rate schedules for individuals include joint returns for married couples, single returns, and head of household returns for single individuals with dependents. Married couples can file separate returns; the brackets in these schedules are half as wide as brackets in the joint return, so there is no tax rate advantage in filing such a return. The individual income tax rate schedules for 2010 are shown in Table 2. In the absence of legislative action, the current marginal tax rates will revert back to year 2000 levels after the 2010 tax year.[17]

As was noted above, income earned from long-term capital gains and dividends is taxed at lower rates. For tax years 2008 through 2010, capital gains and dividends are taxed at 15% for most taxpayers. Taxpayers in the 10% and 15% tax brackets have a tax rate of 0% on capital gains and dividends for tax years 2008 through 2010. In the absence of further legislative action, long-term capital gains will be taxed at a rate of 20% (10% for taxpayers in the 15% bracket) and dividends will be taxed as ordinary income after 2010.

Given the complexities of the tax code, most taxpayers do not pay the marginal tax rates associated with their tax bracket. Various tax provisions are available to individuals depending on their level of income. For example, the earned income tax credit (EITC) phases in as income increases, reducing a taxpayer's marginal tax rate. At higher income levels, as the credit phases out, the taxpayer faces a higher marginal tax rate during that phase out range.

Table 2. Statutory Marginal Tax Rates, 2010

Married Filing Jointly			
If taxable income is:			Then, tax is:
$ 0	to	$16,750	10% of the amount over $0
$16,700	to	$68,000	$ 1,675 plus 15% of the amount over $16,700
$68,000	to	$137,300	$ 9,362.50 plus 25% of the amount over $68,000
$137,300	to	$209,250	$26,687.50 plus 28% of the amount over $137,300
$209,250	to	$373,650	$46,833.50 plus 33% of the amount over $209,250
$373,650	plus		$101,085.50 plus 35% of the amount over $373,650
Single Returns			
If taxable income is:			Then, tax is:
$0	to	$8,375	10% of the amount over $0
$8,375	to	$34,000	$837.50 plus 15% of the amount over $8,375
$34,000	to	$82,400	$4,681.25 plus 25% of the amount over $34,000
$82,400	to	$171,850	$16,781.25 plus 28% of the amount over $82,400
$171,850	to	$373,650	$41,827.25 plus 33% of the amount over $171,850
$373,650	plus		$108,421.25 plus 35% of the amount over $373,650
Heads of Households			
If taxable income is:			Then, tax is:
$0	to	$11,950	10% of the amount over $0
$11,950	to	$45,550	$1,195 plus 15% of the amount over $11,950
$45,550	to	$117,650	$6,235 plus 25% of the amount over $45,550
$117,650	to	$190,550	$24,260 plus 28% of the amount over $117,650
$190,550	to	$373,650	$44,672 plus 33% of the amount over $190,550
$373,650	plus		$105,095 plus 35% of the amount over $373,650

Source: Internal Revenue Code.

Higher-income individuals with a high ratio of exemptions and deductions to income may be subject to the alternative minimum tax (AMT). There are two marginal tax rates under the AMT, 26% and 28%, that are applied to an expanded base. The AMT is discussed in further detail below.

Tax Credits

Tax credits offset tax liability on a dollar-for-dollar basis. Over time, tax credits have become an increasingly popular method of providing tax relief and social benefits. There are two different types of tax credits: those that are refundable and those that are non-refundable. If a tax credit is refundable, and the credit amount exceeds tax liability, a taxpayer receives a payment from the government. The earned income credit is refundable, and the child tax credit is refundable for all but very low-income families. If credits are not refundable, then the credit is limited to the amount of tax liability. Non-refundable credits provide limited benefits to many middle- and lower-income individuals who have little or no tax liability. Many credits are phased out as income rises and thus do not benefit higher income individuals. These phaseout points vary considerably across different credits. Tax credits are available for a wide variety of purposes. The major individual income tax credits are described below.

Child Tax Credit

The credit for taxpayers with children under 17 was adopted in 1997 and was originally set at $400 for each qualifying child. Subsequent legislation in 2001, 2003, and 2004 increased the credit to $1,000 and made the credit partially refundable. Legislation in 2008 and 2009 temporarily expanded eligibility for the refundable portion of the credit.[18] In 2010, families may qualify for a $1,000 credit per qualifying child. This credit is phased out for higher income families.

Dependent Care Credit

This credit is provided for the costs of paid care for dependents, mostly children. The maximum credit rate is 35% of costs. The value of the credit is capped at $3,000 for one dependent and $6,000 for two or more dependents. The rate is reduced when the taxpayer's adjusted gross income (AGI) exceeds $15,000, but is no less than 20% for higher-income taxpayers. The credit is nonrefundable.[19] The current credit amounts were set under EGTRRA. Absent legislative action, the maximum credit amounts will fall to $2,400 for one child, and $4,800 for two children, beginning after 2010.

Earned Income Tax Credit

The earned income tax credit (EITC) supplements wages for lower-income families and individuals. Since the 1990s, the EITC has been a major component of the federal government's poverty reduction strategy and is currently the largest anti-poverty cash entitlement program. The EITC is refundable (otherwise, it could not fulfill its function) and is phased out at lower and moderate income levels.[20]

Hope and Lifetime Learning Credits (Education Credits)

The Hope credit is limited to $2,500 per student for 2009 and 2010 for expenditures on tuition (temporarily increased from $1,200 and temporarily allows expenditures related to tuition to qualify), and is available for the first four years of college (temporarily extended from the first two). The Hope credit is temporarily partially refundable for 2009 and 2010 (prior to 2009 the credit was non-refundable) and phases out for higher-income individuals. Presently, the Lifetime Learning credit rate is 20% of costs up to $10,000 for qualified tuition and related expenses. The credit is capped at $2,000. The Lifetime Learning credit is nonrefundable.[21]

Alternative Minimum Tax

Individuals may also pay tax under the alternative minimum tax (AMT). Under current law, to calculate the AMT, an individual first adds back various tax items, including personal exemptions and certain itemized deductions, to regular taxable income. This grossed up amount becomes the income base for the AMT. Next, an exemption of $70,950 for joint returns and $46,700 for single and head of household returns is subtracted from this income base to obtain AMT taxable income. (These exemption levels are temporary levels for 2009, and are scheduled to revert to their prior law levels of $45,000 for joint returns and $35,750 for unmarried taxpayers in 2010.) The basic exemptions are phased out for taxpayers with high levels of AMT income. A two-tiered rate structure of 26% and 28% is then assessed against AMT taxable income. The taxpayer compares his AMT tax liability to his regular tax liability and pays the greater of the two.

Even taxpayers that do not actually pay the AMT may see their regular tax liability affected by the AMT. Nonrefundable tax credits under the regular income tax are limited to the excess of regular income tax over AMT liability. Thus, a taxpayer who has a net $4,000 regular income tax liability ($5,000 tax liability less $1,000 in nonrefundable tax credits) but has an AMT liability of $4,300 will, effectively, see his regular income tax credits reduced by $300. Temporary provisions, first enacted in 1998, allow individuals to use all personal tax credits against both their regular and AMT tax liabilities.[22]

Although the AMT was originally designed to prevent high-income taxpayers from escaping what was perceived to be their fair share of the income tax burden, since the exemption amounts are not indexed to inflation, there will be a significant increase in the number of middle- to uppermiddle-income taxpayers affected by the AMT in the absence of legislation to increase the exemption amounts or broader reform.[23]

The Corporate Income Tax

Table 3 contains the marginal corporate tax rates faced by U.S. firms. Smaller firms face a progressive tax schedule. The tax schedule was designed so that most firms face an effective tax rate of 35%. In order to increase the effective tax rate for larger firms, the statutory rate increases above 35% for two brackets: the 39% bracket for income between $100,000 and $335,000 and the 38% bracket for income between $15,000,000 and $18,333,333. Having these "bubble" rates, or higher marginal tax rates along part of the schedule, increases the effective tax rate for higher-income corporations. Essentially, these higher "bubble" brackets serve to reduce any tax savings larger corporations would have incurred from having their first $75,000 in income taxed at lower rates.

The base of the corporate income tax is net income, or profits, as defined by the tax code. In general this is gross revenue less the cost of doing business. Deductible costs include materials, interest, and wage payments. Another important deductible cost is depreciation—an allowance for declines in the value of a firm's tangible assets, such as machines, equipment, and structures.

In broad economic terms, the base of the corporate income tax is the return to equity capital. Wages are tax deductible, so labor's contribution to corporate revenue is excluded from the corporate tax base. Income produced by corporate capital investment includes that produced by corporate investment of borrowed funds, and that produced by investment of equity, or funds provided by stockholders. Profits from debt-financed investment are paid out as interest, which is deductible. Thus, the return to debt capital is excluded from the corporate tax base. Equity investments are financed by retained earnings and the sale of stock. The income equity investment generates is paid out as dividends and the capital gains that accrue as stock increases in value. Neither form of income is generally deductible. Thus, the base of the corporate income tax is the return to equity capital.

Table 3. Corporate Tax Rate Schedule, 2010
Taxable Corporate Income Corporate Tax Rate

$0-$49,999	15%
$50,000-$74,999	25%
$75,000-$99,999	34%
$100,000-$334,999	39%
$335,000-$9,999,999	34%
$10,000,000-$14,999,999	35%
$15,000,000-$18,333,332	38%
$18,333,333 and over	35%

Source: IRS.

Notes: Like the individual income tax, the corporate tax schedule contains marginal tax rates. All firms, no matter what their level of taxable income, pay a 15% income tax rate on the first $50,000 of taxable income.

Because of the nature of its base, the corporate income tax has several broad effects on the allocation of capital investment. First, it favors non-corporate investment—for example, unincorporated business and owner-occupied housing—over corporate investment. Second, it favors corporate debt over corporate equity investment since the former is not subject to the tax.

However, while the base of the tax is equity income, the flow of capital out of the corporate sector and other economic adjustments probably cause the burden of the tax to spread to all owners of capital: owners of unincorporated business, bondholders, and homeowners. The tax can also shift from capital income to labor income, or even benefit labor income (with capital bearing more than 100% of the tax). The government agencies that provide distributional analysis allocate the corporate tax to capital in general.

In evaluating the corporate tax, it is useful to ask why corporate profits are subject to separate taxation. Corporate equity profits are taxed twice, once at the corporate level and once under the individual income tax when they are received by stockholders as dividends or capital gains. As a consequence, taxes tend to steer investment away from the corporate sector. Further, corporations are not persons who can bear the burden of taxes, but merely legal entities through which individuals earn income. From this point of view, it is misleading to compare the tax burden of a corporation with that of an individual. The corporate tax, some argue, should be combined ("integrated") with the individual income tax in some manner.

On the other hand, there are arguments for maintaining the current tax structure where corporate profits are subject to a separate tax. First, it discourages the use of corporations as shelters from the individual income tax. Second, it likely enhances the tax system's progressivity. Third, integration of the individual and corporate taxes would present administrative difficulties. Fourth, the corporate tax has a degree of public support. Finally, the corporate tax also raises significant revenue.

In 2003, the Jobs and Growth Tax Relief Reconciliation Act (JGTRRA) took measures intended to relieve the double-taxation of corporate income by reducing the tax rate individuals pay on corporate-source dividends and capital gains to 15% for 2003 to 2008. In 2006, the Tax Increase Prevention Reconciliation Act (TIPRA) extended the reduced rates through 2010.[24]

Payroll Taxes

Payroll taxes are used to fund specific programs, largely Social Security and Medicare. Social Security and Medicare taxes make up the largest share of federal payroll taxes by a wide margin. Social Security and Medicare taxes are paid at a combined rate of 15.3% of wages, with 7.65% being paid by the employee and employer alike. In 2010, the Social Security part of the tax (6.2% for both employees and employers) is only levied on the first $106,800 of wages, with the cap adjusted annually for increases in average wages in the economy. The Medicare portion (2.9%) is applied to all wages.[25]

The other categories of federal payroll taxes are unemployment insurance taxes (FUTA) and employees' contributions to the federal retirement system. The federal portion of the unemployment tax is applied at a 6.2% rate to the first $7,000 of wages. However, the states apply the tax at a 5.4% rate that is credited against the federal tax so that the net federal rate is 0.8%.

Estate and Gift Tax

The federal estate tax is imposed when property is transferred at death. The taxable unit is the estate, in contrast to an inheritance tax, which is levied on heirs. The base of the federal estate tax is property transferred at death, less allowable deductions and exemptions. The base is subject to graduated rates that rise from

18% to 45% as estate size increases. An unlimited marital deduction is allowed for property transferred to a surviving spouse. Other allowable deductions include estate administration expenses, transfers to charity, and certain other items. A tax credit (the unified credit) is allowed against the tentative estate tax liability, which has the effect of exempting the first $3.5 million of an estate from tax in 2009. Under the provisions of the Economic Growth and Tax Relief Reconciliation Act of 2001 (EGTRRA; P.L. 107-16), the estate tax is repealed in 2010. Since the provisions of EGTRRA sunset after 2010, in 2011 the estate tax is scheduled to return to rates scheduled prior to EGTRRA (a tax credit effectively exempting the first $1 million of estate from tax and having a top tax rate of 55%).

The federal gift tax operates alongside the estate tax to prevent individuals from avoiding the estate tax by transferring property to heirs before dying. (Note that the first $13,000 of gifts from one individual to another is excluded from taxation in 2009. Thus, a married couple could each give a child $13,000 for a total gift of $26,000.) The gift and estate taxes are unified because the same rates and unified credit amount apply to the cumulative taxable transfers over an individual's lifetime and at death. For example, a gift tax credit of $25,000 claimed during a person's lifetime reduces the credit that can be claimed at death under the estate tax by $25,000. The rate bracket that applies to a transfer at death is based on cumulative gifts over the decedent's lifetime as well as the size of the estate. EGTRRA gradually reduces the top rate of the gift tax parallel to the estate tax reductions. The gift tax will remain in place after 2010; its top rate will be the top individual income tax rate applicable under EGTRRA.

The estate and gift tax occupies a minor role in the federal fiscal structure, accounting for 1.1% of gross federal tax collections in FY2008.[26] Further, because of the exemption (the unified credit) and deductions, few estates pay the tax. In 2007, 0.6% of deaths resulted in any estate tax liability. Since the exemption is higher in 2009 than in 2007, it is expected that even fewer deaths, approximately 0.2%, will result in estate tax liability in 2009.[27]

Aside from raising revenue, the estate tax has been defended as a means of increasing the overall progressivity of the tax system. The tax falls on those with the greatest wealth, and wealth is widely regarded as a good measure of an individual's ability to pay. Some have argued, however, that the tax impairs operation of the economy by discouraging lifetime saving and capital formation. Whether the estate tax does so, however, is unclear.

The possible impact of the estate tax on small business and farms has often been the subject of debate. Some have argued, for example, that the tax inhibits the transfer of farms and small businesses to heirs and prevents them from staying in the decedent's family. As a result of such concerns, the estate tax currently has a number of special rules designed to ease its burden on farms and small businesses. However, tax return data show that the farm and business estates most likely to dispose of assets to pay the estate tax tend to be larger estates.[28]

Excise Taxes

Excise taxes are a form of consumption tax—levied on the consumption of goods and services rather than income. Unlike sales taxes, they apply to particular commodities, rather than to broad categories. While the federal government has left sales taxes to the states as a revenue source, it levies a variety of excise taxes.[29] Federal excise tax revenues are small compared to other federal taxes. In FY2009, $62.5 billion in excise taxes were collected, amounting to 3% of total federal receipts.[30]

Federal excise taxes are levied on a variety of products. The collection point of the tax varies across products; for some goods taxes are collected at the production level while other excise taxes are collected on retail sales. In terms of receipts, the single largest tax is the excise tax on gasoline, which made up 36.3% of all excise tax receipts in FY2008.[31] Other prominent excise taxes are those on diesel fuel, domestic air passengers, distilled spirits, beer, cigarettes, and telephone services.

Most federal excise taxes are paid into trust funds devoted to various federal activities rather than remaining in the federal budget's general fund. In FY2009, 78% of excise tax receipts went into trust funds.[32] The largest amount went into the Highway Trust Fund, and consisted of highway motor fuels taxes (including the gasoline tax), retail sales taxes on tractors and heavy trucks and trailers, and an annual heavy vehicle use tax.

Excise taxes serve a variety of fiscal purposes. Some were enacted simply to raise revenue (for example, the telephone tax and fuel taxes were enacted for deficit reduction). The taxes linked with trust funds serve to fund expenditure programs by taxing their beneficiaries, or by taxing those responsible for certain problems addressed by expenditure programs. Some excise taxes adjust for the effects of negative externalities—that is, they seek to ensure that the price of products that produce side-effects like the consumption of alcohol and tobacco reflects their true cost to society. Other purposes of excise taxes include adjusting the price of imports to reflect domestic taxes and regulation of activities thought to be undesirable.

The burden of excise taxes is thought to fall on consumption and more heavily on individuals with lower incomes. The tax is believed to be usually passed on by producers to consumers in the form of higher prices. Because consumption is a higher proportion of income for lower-income persons than upper-income individuals, excise taxes are usually considered regressive. However, the incidence of excise taxes in particular cases depends on the market conditions, and how consumers and producers respond to price changes. Further, some economists have argued that consideration of the incidence of excise taxes over an individual's lifetime reduces their apparent regressivity. The effects of excise taxes on economic efficiency vary, depending on the particular tax. For example, taxes that counter negative externalities probably enhance economic efficiency. On the other hand, excise taxes that reduce economic welfare by distorting prices and consumption choices likely reduce efficiency.[33]

Tax Statistics

Composition and Size of the Federal Tax System

The federal tax system is composed of five major sources of tax revenue. In FY2009 the individual income tax accounted for 44% of total federal revenue, the Social Security tax for 42% of total revenue, the corporate income tax for 7% of the total, and excise taxes for approximately 3% of the total.[34] The remaining 5% was collected through the estate and gift tax, customs duties, and other taxes.

Figure 2 displays federal tax revenues as a percentage of gross domestic product (GDP). Since the 1960s, total federal revenues have fluctuated between 16% and 21% of (GDP), with the average over the period approximately 18% of GDP. After reaching a post-World War II peak of nearly 21% of GDP in FY2000, federal receipts measured as a percentage of GDP declined to a 53-year low of 16% of GDP in FY2004. Revenues as a percent of GDP were relatively low, less than 15% in FY2009, as compared to the historical average. Revenues as a percentage of GDP are expected to remain at this level in FY2010 before increasing toward the historical average.

Since the mid-1940s, the individual income tax has been the most important source of federal revenue. Since 2000, however, the individual income tax receipts have decreased from more than 10% of GDP to just over 6% in 2009. Over time, the corporate income tax has fallen from the second to the third most important source of revenue. In the late 1960s, corporate taxes were replaced by Social Security taxes as the second leading revenue source. Excise taxes have also decreased in relative importance over time.

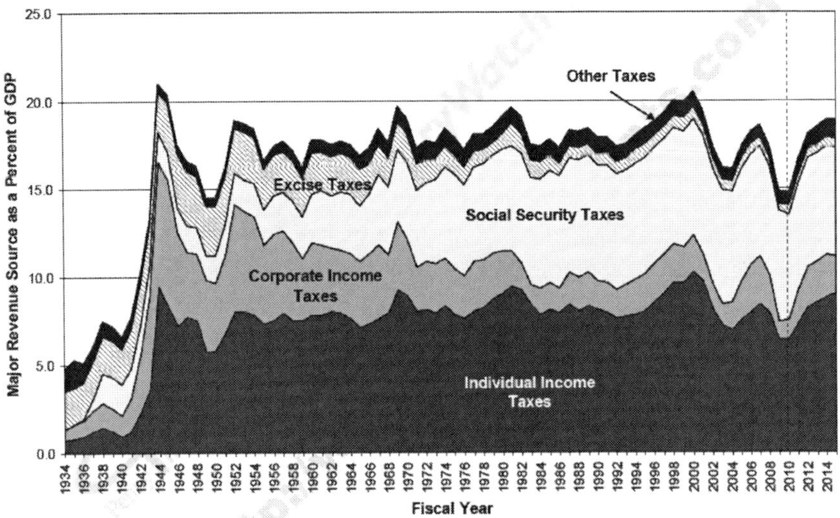

Source: CRS calculations using data from U.S. Office of Management and Budget, *Budget of the U.S. Government, Fiscal Year 2011, Historical Tables* (Washington: GPO, 2010). Table 2.3. http://www.whitehouse.gov/omb/budget/Historicals.

Notes: Revenues for 2010-2015 are projections. FY2010 is noted with the vertical dotted line.

Figure 2. Federal Revenue as a Percentage of GDP, 1934 – 2015.

The U.S. Fiscal Position Compared to Other Nations

The U.S. budget deficit as a percentage of GDP has increased in recent years. Budget deficits averaged 1.5% of GDP between 2000 and 2008. These deficits began increasing in 2008, reaching nearly 10% of GDP in 2009.[35]

Given congressional interest in the fiscal position of the federal government, the question of how the U.S. public sector compares to other nations often arises. Using aggregate budget data for all levels of government relative to economic output (budget aggregates as a percentage of gross domestic product, GDP) as one measure of the size of public sectors, several observations can be made.

- Compared with the other major industrialized nations, the public sector (including all levels of government) in the United States is relatively small.
- In terms of revenue, Japan and the U.S. public sectors collect the least amount of revenue relative to their economic output.

- In terms of outlays, the U.S. public sector has a relatively low level of outlays relative to its economic output.

Table 4 presents Organization for Economic Cooperation and Development (OECD) estimates of government revenues, expenditures, and deficits/surpluses as a percentage of GDP for the seven major industrialized countries in 2009. Like the U.S., other industrialized countries have experienced rising budget deficits as a result of the recent economic downturn.

Table 4. U.S. Fiscal Position Compared to Other Industrialized Nations, 2009

	Government Revenues as a % of GDP	Government Expenditures as a % of GDP	Surplus/Deficit as a % of GDP
Japan	34.4%	41.5%	-7.2%
United States	30.5	41.5	-11.0
Canada	38.7	43.8	-5.1
United Kingdom	40.2	51.4	-11.3
Germany	44.3	47.6	-3.3
Italy	46.7	51.9	-5.2
France	48.1	55.7	-7.6

Source: OECD Economic Outlook 2010, No. 87 Annex Tables. Available at http://www.oecd.org/document/61/ 0,3343,en_2649_34573_2483901_1_1_1_1,00.html.

Notes: U.S. data exclude the operating surplus of public enterprises.

Distribution of the U.S. Federal Tax Burden Across Income Classes

The distribution of the federal tax burden is a perennial topic of concern and debate. Tax burdens could be distributed such that all taxpayers pay the same percentage of their income in taxes regardless of their income level, a proportional distribution. Alternatively, the tax burden could be distributed such that lower income taxpayers pay a higher percentage of their income in taxes than do upper-income taxpayers, a regressive distribution. Or the tax burden could be distributed progressively such that taxes as a percentage of income increase as incomes increase.

Economic theory does not provide an answer as to how the tax burden should be distributed among people with unequal incomes. While few would argue that the tax system should be regressive, the degree to which it should be progressive involves subjective value judgments. A consensus seems to have evolved that the federal tax system should be progressive, a goal that, over time, has been achieved. Economists refer to this notion as vertical equity—the principle that those with a greater ability to pay taxes (higher income or higher wealth) should pay more.

Table 5 shows that effective tax rates fell for all income groups between 1997 and 2007. In relative terms, effective tax rates declined more for the lowest income quintile (effective tax rate fell by 31%) than for the highest income quintile (effective tax rate fell by 10%). As a result, higher income groups paid a larger share of federal tax liabilities in 2007 than in 1997. The positive effective tax rates for those in the lowest income quintile are driven by payroll taxes.[36]

Table 5. Average Federal Tax Rates for All Households: 1997 and 2007

Income category	Effective Tax Rate 1997	Share of Tax Liabilities 1997	Effective Tax Rate 2007	Share of Tax Liabilities 2007
Lowest quintile	5.8%	1.1%	4.0%	0.8%
Second quintile	13.6	5.4	10.6	4.4
Middle quintile	17.4	10.8	14.3	9.2
Fourth quintile	20.5	18.3	17.4	16.5
Highest quintile	28.0	64.2	25.1	68.9
Top 10%	29.9	49.3	26.7	55.0
Top 5%	31.6	38.3	27.9	44.3
Top 1%	34.9	22.7	29.5	28.1
All quintiles	22.9	100.0	20.4	100.0

Source: U.S. Congress, Congressional Budget Office, *Average Federal Taxes by Income Group* (June 2010). Available at http://www.cbo.gov/publications/collections/collections.cfm?collect=13.

Selected Tax Concepts

The final sections of this report review a number of important tax concepts. First, tax expenditures are discussed. Tax expenditures represent revenue losses from tax deductions, credits, and other tax benefits. Tax expenditures are used to provide incentives or disincentives regarding various behavior via the tax code. Capital gains are reviewed in further detail, as there is ongoing debate surrounding the preferred tax treatment of this form of income. The tax consequences of marriage are also discussed. While marriage tax penalties have been reduced in recent years, the possibility that marriage can change a couple's tax liability still exists. The concepts of tax deferral and depreciation are also reviewed, as changes in policies here can have broad implications for tax liability. The final sections note how forms of business organization can impact tax liability, and assess the possibility of tax policy enhancing firm or industry competitiveness.

Tax Expenditures

Tax expenditures are revenue losses from special tax deductions, credits, and other tax benefits. The Joint Committee on Taxation lists revenue losses from these tax provisions by functional spending categories. Table 6 lists the top 10 individual tax expenditures. These 10 expenditure categories account for 70% of total tax expenditures on individuals. The largest tax expenditure is allowing dividends and long-term capital gains to be taxed at reduced rates, resulting in a loss of revenue of $150.2 billion for 2008. Excluding employer-provided health care from tax results in a loss of tax revenue of $116.8 billion for 2008.

Table 7 reports estimated total tax expenditures for individuals and corporations for FY2008 through FY2012. While it is not precisely correct to add up all tax expenditures, which are estimated individually and have some interactive effects, these totals provide some notion of the magnitude of these provisions. In FY2008, individual income taxes yielded $1,145.7 billion.[37] Thus, tax expenditures are large relative to total receipts.

It is also important to note that tax expenditures measure the revenue effects of provisions on a cash flow basis, so they may not reflect the true benefit to the taxpayer (e.g., when the value of a benefit arises from a deferral of taxes). The initial revenue effects of a repeal of a provision may differ from the costs reflected in the tax expenditure budget.

Table 6. 10 Largest Tax Expenditures for Individuals, 2008
Billions of Dollars

Tax Expenditure	Amount
Reduced rates of tax on dividends and long-term capital gains	150.2
Exclusion of contributions and earnings to retirement plans	119.2
Exclusion of employer contributions for health care	116.8
Recovery rebate	95.0
Deduction for mortgage interest	67.0
Earned income tax credit	48.6
Deduction of state and local taxes	48.0
Tax credit for children under age 17	47.6
Deduction for charitable contributions	44.3
Exclusion of Medicare benefits	41.0

Source: U.S. Congress, Senate, Committee on the Budget, *Tax Expenditures – Compendium of Background Material on Individual Provisions,* December 2008, p.7; updated biennially by CRS with revenue data provided by the Joint Committee on Taxation.

Table 7. Sum of Tax Expenditures: FY2008-FY2012
Billions of Dollars

Fiscal Year	Individuals	Corporations	Total
2008	1,014.6	118.1	1,222.7
2009	1,047.3	117.0	1,164.3
2010	1,060.6	99.4	1,160.0
2011	1,106.0	105.9	1,211.9
2012	1,166.2	116.0	1,282.2

Source: U.S. Congress, Senate, Committee on the Budget, *Tax Expenditures – Compendium of Background Material on Individual Provisions,* December 2008, p.13; updated biennially by CRS with revenue data provided by the Joint Committee on Taxation.

Capital Gains

Under current income tax law, a capital gain or loss can result from the sale or exchange of a capital asset. If the asset is sold for a higher price than its acquisition price, then the sale produces a capital gain. If the asset is sold for a lower price than its acquisition price, then the sale produces a capital loss. The tax rate on capital gains taxes was reduced in 1997. Under current law, capital assets held for more than 12 months are considered long-term assets, while assets held 12 months or less are considered short-term assets. The holding period to qualify for longterm capital gain tax treatment was reduced in 1998. Capital gains on short-term assets are taxed at regular income tax rates. In 2003, the Jobs and Growth Tax Relief Reconciliation Act (JGTRRA) reduced the maximum tax rate on long-term capital gains income. For 2008 through 2010, the tax rate on capital gains is 0% for those in the 10% and 15% tax brackets. JGTRRA reduced the maximum capital gains tax rate to 15% for taxpayers in marginal income tax brackets exceeding 15%. These changes were initially effective for assets sold or exchanged on or after May 6, 2003, and before January 1, 2009, but the Tax Increase Prevention and Reconciliation Act of 2006 (P.L. 109-222) extended the applicability of reduced rates through 2010.

Some economists argue that lowering capital gains taxes would significantly reduce "lock-in" effects, allowing capital to flow more freely to where it can be used most efficiently. Reducing capital gains taxes could lead to more capital gains realizations, potentially offsetting some of the cost of cutting capital gains taxes. There is, however, considerable uncertainty about the magnitude of this unlocking effect. As an alternative to reduced capital gains tax rates, lock-in could be reduced by taxing capital gains on an accrual basis (as opposed to the current system, which taxes capital gains when they are realized) or by taxing capital gains passed on at death. These alternative solutions, however, face a variety of technical problems, and the idea of taxing gains at death has been unpopular.

Arguments have also been made that cutting capital gains taxes could increase savings and stimulate economic growth. While evidence on the effect of tax cuts on savings rates and, thus, economic growth is difficult to obtain, most evidence does not indicate a large response of savings to an increase in the after-tax rate of return on assets. Further, many economists argue that reduced capital gains tax rates are unlikely to provide short-run economic stimulus.

A case might be made for cutting capital gains taxes on corporate stock since corporate equity capital is subject to taxation both under the corporate and individual income taxes. This double taxation encourages corporations to take on debt and directs capital to the non-corporate sector. On the other hand, reducing the capital gains tax would increase the relative penalty that applies to dividends and introduce tax distortions into the decisions of firms to retain earnings.

A major complaint made by some is that cutting capital gains taxes would primarily benefit very high-income individuals. Capital gains are concentrated among higher-income individuals both because these individuals tend to own capital and because they are especially likely to own capital that generates capital gains income.[38]

Marriage Penalties and Bonuses

Defining the married couple as a single tax unit under the federal individual income tax violates the principle of marriage neutrality. Some married couples pay more income tax than they would as two unmarried singles (a marriage tax penalty) while other married couples pay less income tax than they would as two unmarried singles (a marriage tax bonus). This can be viewed as a violation of the principle of horizontal equity, whereby individuals with equal income should have similar tax burdens.

The most important structural factors affecting the marriage neutrality of the income tax are the earned income tax credit (EITC), the marginal tax rate schedules, and the phaseout of credits and deductions for higher-income individuals. Under the current tax system, single individuals, heads of households, and married couples are subject to tax rate schedules.[39] In addition, the EITC amounts and phaseout ranges vary based on the number of dependents claimed. These differences give rise to structural marriage tax bonuses and penalties.

Generally, the more evenly divided the earned income of the two spouses, the more likely they are to have a structural marriage tax penalty. Hence, married couples in which each spouse earns 50% of the total earned income have the largest marriage tax penalties. Specifically, two individuals having $80,000 each in taxable income would be in the 25% marginal tax bracket when being taxed as individuals. Their federal income tax liability would be $16,181.25 each (or $32,362.50 jointly). However, were these same persons taxed as a married couple, they would be in the 28% marginal tax bracket and have a joint federal income tax liability of $33,043.50. The marriage tax penalty for this couple would be $681.

On the other hand, married couples where one spouse earns all the earned income have the largest marriage tax bonuses. For example, an individual with a taxable income of $100,000 would have a federal income tax liability of $21,709.25. If that individual took a spouse who had no earnings, the tax liability for a couple with $100,000 in taxable income is $17,362.50. Hence, this couple would have a marriage tax bonus of $4,346.75.

In 2003, the Jobs and Growth Tax Relief Reconciliation Act (JGTRRA) accelerated provisions initially introduced in the Economic Growth and Tax Relief Reconciliation Act of 2001 (EGTRRA; P.L. 107-16) aimed to reduce the marriage tax penalty. Specifically, the 2001 and 2003 legislation made the standard deduction for married couples filing jointly twice that of the standard deduction for individuals. The 2001 and 2003 legislation also increased the 15% bracket for married couples filing jointly to extend to twice the income level as for single individuals. Both of these measures were initially temporary for the 2003 and 2004 tax years but were extended through 2010 by the Working Family Tax Relief Act of 2004 (WFTRA). While these changes did reduce the marriage tax penalty for some, higher-income couples and low- to middle-income couples with children are still likely to face a marriage tax penalty.[40]

It is widely accepted that achieving equity in the individual income tax should involve (1) not influencing the choice of individuals regarding their marital status, (2) being progressive, and (3) taxing couples with equal income (whether that income comes from one or two earners) equally. Regardless of how these three concepts of equity are juggled, under current definitions an income tax can achieve only two of the goals; it cannot simultaneously achieve all three. The current income tax has chosen progressivity and equal taxation of couples with equal incomes at the expense of marriage neutrality. A critical point in this debate is that there are no unambiguous right or wrong answers to the question of which of these three competing goals of equity is the most important.

Tax Deferral

One perplexing problem associated with taxing income involves the issue of tax deferral. Ideally, a tax levied on income should be assessed when the income accrues to the taxpayer. However, as a result of many factors, taxes are often deferred into the future. This can happen when income is taxed when it is realized, rather than when it accrues or when there is a mismatch between when income is earned and the expenses associated with earning that income. Since money has a time value (a dollar today is more valuable than a dollar in the future), tax deferral effectively lowers the tax rate on the income in question.

Income from capital gains can be used to illustrate the benefits of tax deferral. For capital gains, the tax is assessed when the gain is realized rather than as it accrues. If a capital asset is acquired for $100 and appreciates at a rate of 10% per annum, by the end of the first year it has appreciated in value to $110 and by the end of the second year it is worth $121. Assuming a marginal tax rate of 15% (the top marginal tax rate on long-term capital gains), if the gain were realized at the end of the second year, then a tax of $3.15 ($21 times 15%) would be levied on the realized appreciation. The after-tax return would be $17.85.

In contrast is the case of a $100 investment in an interest-bearing account earning a 10% rate of return with no deferral. At the end of the first year, the account would yield $10 in interest. Tax on the interest, assuming a 15% marginal income tax rate, would be $1.50, leaving $108.50 in the account. By the end of the second year, the account would yield $10.85 in interest. Tax on the second year's interest would be $1.63, leaving $117.72 in the account, for an after-tax return over the two-year period of $17.72.

It is apparent from the examples above that the investment in the asset yielding capital gains income earns a higher after-tax return than the comparable investment in an interest-bearing account. In essence, the reason for this result is simply that, for the asset producing a capital gain, the tax on the appreciation in the first year was deferred, with the deferred tax remaining in the account and earning interest. The benefits of tax deferral increase the longer an asset is held and tax can be deferred.

Tax deferral not only affects the taxation of assets producing capital gains income, but also is of concern in other areas of tax policy, such as the taxation of contributions to retirement accounts, depreciation allowances, and the taxation of foreign source income of U.S. multinational corporations.

DEPRECIATION

When a business purchases a tangible asset such as a machine or structure, it is not incurring a cost. Rather, the business is simply exchanging one asset—for example, cash—for another. The full purchase price of an asset is therefore usually not tax deductible in the year the asset is bought. Assets do, however, decline in value as they age or become outmoded. This decline in value (depreciation) *is* a cost. Because assets gradually depreciate until they are worthless, the tax code permits firms gradually to deduct the full acquisition cost of an asset over a number of years.

The tax code contains a set of rules that govern the rate at which depreciation deductions can be claimed. The rules determine the tax depreciation rate by specifying a *recovery period* and a *depreciation method* for different types of assets. An asset's recovery period is the number of years over which deductions for the asset's full cost must be spread. The applicable depreciation method determines how depreciation deductions are distributed among the different years of the recovery period. The slowest method is straight-line, in which equal deductions are taken each year. Declining balance methods, in which a fixed fraction of the cost less prior depreciation is deducted, cause larger shares to be taken in earlier years.

Because of the time value of money, a tax deduction of a given dollar amount is worth more to a business the sooner it can be claimed. Further, the sooner a tax deduction can be claimed, the sooner the tax savings it generates can be invested and earn a return. It follows that the tax rules governing when depreciation deductions can be claimed are quite important to businesses. If depreciation deductions can be claimed faster than an asset actually declines in value, a tax benefit exists; depreciation is said to be *accelerated*. If, on the other hand, depreciation deductions can be claimed more slowly than the corresponding asset actually depreciates, a tax penalty occurs. Only if depreciation deductions are claimed at the rate an asset actually depreciates do taxes confer neither a tax benefit nor a tax penalty.

According to some estimates, current tax depreciation for some types of equipment is somewhat accelerated compared to economic depreciation. "Bonus" depreciation allowances that recent tax acts have provided for temporary periods may have further accelerated depreciation for certain equipment.[41] Generally, depreciation for most structures is probably not accelerated. Thus, firms have a tax incentive to use more equipment and fewer of other types of assets in their production process than they otherwise would. This influence of taxes in the allocation of capital can reduce economic efficiency.

Forms of Business Organization

The Internal Revenue Code recognizes several different forms of business organization and their tax treatment varies. The principal forms are *C corporations, S corporations, partnerships, and sole proprietorships.*

Apart from taxes, corporations are a legally defined form of business organization, with ownership stakes represented by shares that may or may not be publicly traded. Shareholders' liabilities are limited to their stake in the corporation. The Internal Revenue Code normally subjects corporate profits to the corporate income tax under its subchapter C; corporations subject to income tax are thus often referred to as "C corporations." As explained more fully above, in the report's section on the corporate income tax, the part of C corporation income generated by equity investment is subject to two layers of tax: the corporate income tax and the individual income tax. In contrast, corporations that qualify as "S corporations" are not subject to the corporate income tax. Instead, their net profits are passed on a pro rata basis through to the individual shareholders who are taxed on the profits under the individual income tax. To be classified as an S corporation, the organization may have no more than 100 shareholders.

Taxes aside, partnerships are like corporations in that they have multiple owners. In contrast to corporations, some partnerships convey a liability for debts that is not limited to partners' contributions to the enterprise. Partnerships are also less likely than corporations to be publicly traded, although some forms of partnerships ("master limited partnerships") are. Like S corporations, partnerships are not subject to the corporate income tax; partners are subject to their share of partnership earnings under the individual income tax.

Limited liability companies (LLCs) have some of the characteristics of both partnerships and corporations. Under IRS "check the box" regulations, LLCs can elect to be taxed either as corporations or as partnerships. Other specially defined business entities include real estate investment trusts (REITs), which are required to engage primarily in passive investment in real estate and securities. Qualifying REITs are permitted to deduct dividends they pay to shareholders, which effectively exempts REITs from the corporate income tax. Regulated investment companies (RICs), who invest primarily in securities and distribute most income, are also permitted to deduct dividends. The simplest forms of business organization are sole proprietorships. Sole proprietorships have only one owner; there is no legal distinction between the business and the business's owner. For tax purposes, business profits earned by a sole proprietor are taxed to the owner under the individual income tax. The corporate income tax does not apply.[42]

Taxes and Competitiveness

Competitiveness can be defined in a variety of ways (indeed, some would argue that it has no concrete meaning at all, at least at the national level). But regardless of how competitiveness is defined, standard economic analysis suggests that most tax measures can do little to enhance it. Indeed, some observers argue that many of the tax provisions designed to improve U.S. performance in the world economy actually reduce U.S. economic welfare, world economic welfare, or both.

An individual firm or its employees might defend competitiveness as its ability to withstand the threat of foreign competition. If asked, they might recommend some manner of tax benefit targeted at their industry: perhaps favorable depreciation rules or tax credits for consumers who buy their product. Economic analysis predicts that such measures might well improve the position of the targeted industry: its costs would fall because its taxes have fallen, introducing the possibility of reduced prices, larger market shares, and more jobs.

Economic theory, however, also predicts that the effects of a targeted tax benefit will ripple through the economy and ultimately confound the policy's competitiveness goals for the economy as a whole. Because the nation's resources are limited, the theory holds, a narrowly targeted tax benefit will simply reshuffle the way resources are employed, drawing them into the favored industry and away from alternative uses. While exports in the favored sector may rise (or imports fall), theory predicts that the performance of other sectors will decline. Further, economics predicts that the effect of taxes on how the economy's resources are deployed diminishes the nation's economic vitality: market forces, not tax rules, are usually the best way to guarantee that resources are used efficiently.

Policymakers or others at the national level may take a broader view of competitiveness and define it as the ability of the country as a whole to sell its exports—not just the performance of one sector. Such a view might recommend, for example, a tax incentive for exporting, regardless of the product. But in this case, economic theory suggests that exchange rate adjustments will stymie any effect the export subsidy may have in improving the trade balance. Although implementation of an export subsidy may initially increase exports, the increase in exports raises the price of the dollar in currency markets, which, in turn, makes U.S. exports more expensive and imports cheaper. As a result, exports are predicted to fall and imports increase until any initial improvement in the balance of trade that may have occurred disappears. Further, to the extent that part of the export tax benefit is passed on to foreign consumers as lower prices, analysis indicates that the measure transfers economic welfare from U.S. taxpayers to foreign persons.

Many economists would argue that taxes can alter the balance of trade in the short and medium term, but not in the way that is perhaps commonly thought. If a country runs a trade deficit, it is using more than it produces; and to do so, it must, in effect, borrow from abroad, importing the foreign investment that finances the deficit. The trade balance thus mirrors the balance on capital account, and it follows that taxes alter the trade balance not by their direct application to exports or imports, but by altering capital flows. For example, a cut in taxes on business investment in the United States increases the U.S. appetite for investment; foreign capital inflows accordingly increase and net U.S. exports (imports minus exports) fall. Or, a tax cut that increases the federal budget deficit can be expected to exert upward pressure on real interest rates, thereby attracting additional foreign capital and expanding the trade deficit. Conversely, a tax increase that reduces the budget deficit can also reduce the trade deficit.

Finally, there are questions regarding whether tax preferences on capital rather than trade can enhance competitiveness for U.S. firms. For example, can taxes improve the economy by making U.S. firms that operate abroad more competitive, cutting their costs and helping them compete more effectively against foreign firms? Again, economic theory is doubtful, holding that economic performance is enhanced by a neutral tax policy that neither discourages nor encourages overseas investment.[43]

APPENDIX. 2009 PEP AND PEASE PHASEOUT LIMITS

While PEP and Pease limits do not apply for 2010, limits were in place in 2009 and are expected to return again in 2011. Table A-1 shows the personal exemption phaseout range for 2009. For married couples filing jointly, the personal exemption amount is reduced starting for individuals with an AGI of $250,000. By the time the married couple filing jointly earns $372,000 the value of the personal exemption is zero.

Table A-1. Phase Out of Personal Exemption 2009

Filing Status	Phase Out Starts	Phase Out Ends
Married Filing Jointly	$250,000	$372,700
Single Individual	$166,800	$289,300
Head of Household	$208,500	$331,000

Source: Internal Revenue Code

Notes: For married couples filing separately the phase out range is half the value listed for married couples filing jointly.

In 2009, itemized deductions began to phase out for taxpayers with a filing status of married filing jointly, single individuals, and heads of household at $166,800 and $83,400 for married individuals filing separately. Calculating the reduction is a three-step process. First, the reduction is calculated as the lesser of (1) 3% of AGI in excess of the threshold amount, or (2) 80% of the total amount of otherwise allowable itemized deductions.[44] Second, the amount of the reduction is reduced by two-thirds. Third, the amount from the second step is subtracted from the individual's otherwise allowable itemized deductions to calculate actual allowable itemized deductions.

End Notes

[1] A full list of "above the line" deductions can be found in the Internal Revenue Code (IRC) § 62.

[2] The elderly and blind are allowed an additional standard deduction.

[3] See CRS Report RL32781, *Federal Deductibility of State and Local Taxes*, by Steven Maguire, for analysis of the deductibility of state and local taxes.

[4] If a taxpayer was married and had one child being claimed as a dependent, the exemption would be $10,950 ($3,650 × 3).

[5] See CRS Report R40508, *Personal Exemption Phaseout (PEP) and Limitation on Itemized Deductions (Pease)*, by Maxim Shvedov.

[6] A marginal tax rate is the tax rate on the last dollar earned.

[7] For historical perspective on marginal tax rates see CRS Report RL34498, *Statutory Individual Income Tax Rates and Other Elements of the Tax System: 1988 Through 2010*, by Maxim Shvedov.

[8] See CRS Report R41394, *Tax Treatment of Long-Term Capital Gains and Dividends and Related Provisions in the President's FY2011 Budget Proposal*, by Maxim Shvedov for further information.

[9] The Haig-Simons comprehensive income definition was first developed in Robert Murray Haig, "The Concept of Income – Economic and Legal Aspects," in *The Federal Income Tax*, ed. Robert Murray Haig (New York, NY: Columbia University Press, 1921), pp. 1-28 and Henry C. Simons, *Personal Income Taxation: The Definition of Income as a Problem of Fiscal Policy* (Chicago, IL: University of Chicago Press, 1938). An overview of the concept can be found in Jonathan Gruber, *Public Finance and Public Policy*, 2nd ed. (New York, NY: Worth Publishers, 2007).

[10] For the 2008 through 2010 tax years the tax rate on capital gains for individuals in the 10% and 15% tax brackets is 0%.

[11] For more information see CRS Report 96-769, *Capital Gains Taxes: An Overview*, by Jane G. Gravelle.

[12] For more information see CRS Report RL31597, *The Taxation of Dividend Income: An Overview and Economic Analysis of the Issues*, by Jane G. Gravelle.

[13] Reduced rates for qualified dividends were introduced under Jobs and Growth Tax Relief Reconciliation Act of 2003 (JGTRRA, P.L. 108-27). The reduced rate is set to expire at the end of 2010. For more information, see CRS Report R41394, *Tax Treatment of Long-Term Capital Gains and Dividends and Related Provisions in the President's FY2011 Budget Proposal*, by Maxim Shvedov.

[14] For background on types of business organizations, see CRS Report R40748, *Business Organizational Choices: Taxation and Responses to Legislative Changes*, by Mark P. Keightley.

[15] For further discussion see CRS Report R40508, *Personal Exemption Phaseout (PEP) and Limitation on Itemized Deductions (Pease)*, by Maxim Shvedov.

[16] *Ibid.*

[17] In 2000, marginal tax rates were 15%, 28%, 31%, 36%, and 39.6%. Marginal tax rates were reduced and the 10% bracket introduced under the Economic Growth and Tax Relief Reconciliation Act of 2001 (EGTRRA; P.L. 107-16).

[18] See CRS Report RL34715, *The Child Tax Credit*, by Maxim Shvedov.

[19] See CRS Report RS21466, *Dependent Care: Current Tax Benefits and Legislative Issues*, by Janemarie Mulvey and Christine Scott.

[20] See CRS Report RL31768, *The Earned Income Tax Credit (EITC): An Overview*, by Christine Scott and CRS Report RS21352, *The Earned Income Tax Credit (EITC): Changes for 2009 and 2010*, by Christine Scott.

[21] See CRS Report RL32554, *An Overview of Tax Benefits for Higher Education Expenses*, by Mark P. Keightley and CRS Report RL32507, *Higher Education Tax Credits: An Economic Analysis*, by Mark P. Keightley.

[22] The Economic Growth and Tax Relief Act of 2001 (EGTRRA; P.L. 107-16) contained provisions allowing the child tax credit, the adoption tax credit, and the IRA contribution tax credit to be claimed against a taxpayer's regular income tax liability and AMT tax liability. The EGTRRA provisions expire after 2010.

[23] See CRS Report RL30149, *The Alternative Minimum Tax for Individuals*, by Steven Maguire, for further information.

[24] For more information, see CRS Report RL31597, *The Taxation of Dividend Income: An Overview and Economic Analysis of the Issues*, by Jane G. Gravelle and CRS Report R41394, *Tax Treatment of Long-Term Capital Gains and Dividends and Related Provisions in the President's FY2011 Budget Proposal*, by Maxim Shvedov. For a discussion of who bears the burden of corporate (and other capital) income taxes, see CRS Report RL32517, *Distributional Effects of Taxes on Corporate Profits, Investment Income, and Estates*, by Jane G. Gravelle.

[25] See CRS Report RL32552, *Social Security: Calculation and History of Taxing Benefits*, by Christine Scott and Janemarie Mulvey. For information on policy options involving increasing the payroll tax cap see CRS Report RL33943, *Increasing the Social Security Payroll Tax Base: Options and Effects on Tax Burdens*, by Thomas L. Hungerford.

[26] U.S. Office of Management and Budget, *Budget of the U.S. Government, Fiscal Year 2010, Analytical Perspectives* (Washington: GPO, 2009), p. 279.

[27] Urban Institute and Brookings Institute, Tax Policy Center, *Tax Topics: Estate and Gift Taxes*. Available at http://www.taxpolicycenter.org/taxtopics/estatetax.cfm.

[28] For more information, see CRS Report RL30600, *Estate and Gift Taxes: Economic Issues*, by Donald J. Marples and Jane G. Gravelle; CRS Report RL31061, *Estate and Gift Tax Law: Changes Under the Economic Growth and Tax Relief Reconciliation Act of 2001*, by Nonna A. Noto; and CRS Report RL33070, *Estate Taxes and Family Businesses: Economic Issues*, by Jane G. Gravelle and Steven Maguire.

[29] A national sales tax or a value-added tax has been proposed as alternative or supplementary revenue source. For more information see CRS Report RL33438, *A Value-Added Tax Contrasted With a National Sales Tax*, by James M. Bickley and CRS Report RS22720, *Taxable Base of the Value-Added Tax*, by Maxim Shvedov.

[30] U.S. Office of Management and Budget, *Budget of the U.S. Government, Fiscal Year 2011, Analytical Perspectives* (Washington: GPO, 2009), p. 159. Available at http://www.whitehouse.gov/sites/default/files/ omb/budget/fy2011/ assets/receipts.pdf.

[31] U.S. Internal Revenue Service, *Statistics of Income*, Tax Stats – Historical Table 20. Available at http://www.irs.gov/taxstats/article/0,,id=175900,00.html

[32] U.S. Office of Management and Budget, *Budget of the U.S. Government, Fiscal Year 2011, Analytical Perspectives* (Washington: GPO, 2009), p. 191. Available at http://www.whitehouse.gov/sites/default/files/omb/budget/fy2011/ assets/receipts.pdf.

[33] For more information on the federal excise tax on gasoline see CRS Report R40808, *The Role of Federal Gasoline Excise Taxes in Public Policy*, by Robert Pirog.

[34] U.S. Office of Management and Budget, *Budget of the U.S. Government, Fiscal Year 2011, Historical Tables* Table 2.2 (Washington: GPO, 2010). Available at http://www.whitehouse.gov/omb/budget/Historicals.

[35] These figures are those reported in the President's FY2011 Budget, Historical Tables. These figures may differ from those reported by the OECD.

[36] For further analysis see CRS Report RL32693, *Distribution of the Tax Burden Across Individuals: An Overview*, by Jane G. Gravelle and Maxim Shvedov.

[37] Office of Management and Budget, *Budget of the U.S. Government, Fiscal Year 2010, Analytical Perspectives* (Washington: GPO, 2009), p. 241.

[38] For more information, see CRS Report R40411, *The Economic Effects of Capital Gains Taxation*, by Thomas L. Hungerford and CRS Report 96-769, *Capital Gains Taxes: An Overview*, by Jane G. Gravelle.

[39] Prior to 2003, the standard deduction for married couples filing jointly was less than twice the standard deduction available to individual filers, leading many filers to experience a marriage tax penalty.

[40] U.S. Congress, Senate Committee on Appropriations, Subcommittee on District of Columbia, *The Widespread Prevalance of Marriage Penalties*, Testimony, 109th Cong., 2nd sess., May 3, 2006.

[41] The American Recovery and Reinvestment Act of 2009 (ARRA; P.L. 111-5) contains provisions extending bonus depreciation allowances for certain property. ARRA also contains provisions allowing taxpayers with relatively small levels of investment to expense qualified property. See CRS Report RL31134, *Using Business Tax Cuts to Stimulate the Economy*, by Jane G. Gravelle and CRS Report RL31852, *Small Business Expensing Allowance: Current Status, Legislative Proposals, and Economic Effects*, by Gary Guenther, for more information.

[42] For more information see CRS Report R40748, *Business Organizational Choices: Taxation and Responses to Legislative Changes*, by Mark P. Keightley.

[43] For further information, see CRS Report RS22445, *Taxes and International Competitiveness*, by Donald J. Marples.

[44] For the purposes of calculating 80% of itemized deductions, deductions for medical expenses, investment interest, casualty and theft losses, and wagering losses are excluded.

In: Federal Taxation
Editor: Jaclyn N. Prichard

ISBN: 978-1-61324-102-8

Chapter 2

TAX REFORM: AN OVERVIEW OF PROPOSALS IN THE 112TH CONGRESS*

James M. Bickley

SUMMARY

The President and leading members of Congress have stated that fundamental tax reform is a major policy objective for the 112th Congress. These policymakers have said that fundamental tax reform is needed in order to raise a large amount of additional revenue, which is necessary to reduce high forecast budget deficits and the sharply rising national debt. Congressional interest has been expressed in both a major overhaul of the U.S. tax system and the feasibility of levying a consumption tax. Some proponents of reform argue that the tax base should be broadened by reducing or eliminating many tax expenditures. Tax expenditures are revenue losses resulting from federal tax provisions that grant special tax relief designed to encourage certain kinds of behavior by taxpayers or to aid taxpayers in special circumstances. If tax expenditures are reduced substantially or a consumption tax is levied or both, then the marginal income tax rates could be reduced. An alternative to increasing tax revenues is cutting spending. Thus, members are faced with considering the best mix of tax increases and spending cuts in order to reduce deficits and slow the growth of the national debt.

---

* This is an edited, reformatted and augmented version of Congressional Research Services publication R41591, dated January 14, 2011.

Proposals for fundamental reform have been made in reports by the National Commission on Fiscal Responsibility and Reform (the "Commission") and the Debt Reduction Task Force of the Bipartisan Policy Center. The proposals in these reports may influence the debate over fundamental tax reform. Both proposals recommended the elimination of most tax expenditures and the lowering of marginal corporate and individual income tax rates. In addition, the Debt Reduction Task Force recommended the levying of a 6.5% value-added tax. An evaluation of these and other proposals would consider the effects on equity, efficiency, and simplicity.

A temporary individual AMT patch for 2010 and 2011 was included in the *Tax Relief, Unemployment Insurance Authorization, and Job Creation Act of 2010*, which became P.L. 111-312 on December 17, 2010. The patch increased the individual AMT exemption amounts. Some proponents of tax reform argue that the AMT should be repealed or a permanent patch should be passed. The repeal or passage of a permanent patch of the individual AMT would require a major increase in taxes to offset the large revenue loss.

Options for reforming the federal business income tax are under consideration. The concept of lowering the marginal corporate income tax rate and broadening the corporate income tax base has been advocated by some members of Congress. Other options for reform include corporate tax integration and the replacement of the income tax system with a consumption tax.

The current system of U.S. taxation of international business is complex and difficult to administer. Furthermore, critics argue that the current system is not sufficiently neutral, which results in economic inefficiency. Proposals to reform the system include the replacement of the current hybrid system with either a territorial tax system or a residence-based system.

This report will be updated in the event of significant legislative activity or policy proposals.

INTRODUCTION

The President and leading members of Congress have stated that fundamental tax reform is a major policy objective for the 112th Congress. These policymakers have said that fundamental tax reform is needed in order to raise a large amount of additional revenue, which is necessary to reduce high forecast budget deficits and the sharply rising national debt. Congressional interest has been expressed in both a major overhaul of the U.S. tax system and the feasibility of levying a consumption tax over the existing tax system. Some proponents of reform argue that the tax base should be broadened by reducing or eliminating many tax expenditures. "Tax expenditures are revenue losses resulting from federal tax provisions that grant special tax relief designed to encourage certain kinds of behavior by taxpayers or to aid taxpayers in special circumstances."[1] If tax expenditures are reduced substantially or a consumption tax is levied or both, then the marginal income tax rates could be reduced. An alternative to increasing tax revenues is cutting spending. Thus, members are faced with considering the best mix of tax increases and spending cuts in order to reduce deficits and slow the growth of the national debt.

In December 2010, The National Commission on Fiscal Responsibility and Reform (the "Commission") issued a report titled *The Moment of Truth*, which proposed extensive broadening of both the individual income tax base and the corporate income tax base by eliminating all business tax expenditures and almost all individual tax expenditures.[2] Marginal individual and corporate income tax rates would be reduced, and the individual alternative minimum tax would be abolished. The taxation of foreign-source income would be changed by moving to a territorial system.[3] On November 17, 2010, the Debt Reduction Task Force of the Bipartisan Policy Center issued a report titled *Restoring America's Future*.[4] This report also recommended that individual and corporate income tax bases be broadened by reducing or eliminating most tax expenditures. Marginal individual and corporate income tax rates would be lowered, and the individual alternative minimum tax would be eliminated. In addition, this report recommended that a 6.5% value-added tax be levied. The recommendations of these two reports may influence the tax reform debate in the 112th Congress.

In the 112th Congress, members of Congress are expected to introduce numerous bills containing incremental or marginal adjustments in the tax code in an attempt to redistribute income, reallocate resources, change individual behavior, etc. Proposed incremental or small tax adjustments are considered tax changes.[5] In contrast, fundamental tax reform concerns a major proposed overhaul of the U.S. tax system, which affects the entire tax system or a major component of the system. This report primarily covers fundamental tax reform because CRS reports are available online concerning the other three categories of tax reform: tax reform based on the elimination of the individual alternative minimum tax (AMT), proposals for reforming the corporate income tax, and proposals for reforming the U.S. taxation of international business.[6]

FUNDAMENTAL TAX REFORM OPTIONS

Two broad fundamental tax reform categories for addressing the severe deficit problem are base-broadening and levying a new tax. Some of the revenue from base-broadening and a new tax could be used to reduce marginal tax rates.

Base-Broadening

Some members of Congress have expressed concern about the large number and high cost of tax expenditures.[7] Examples of tax expenditures are the deduction for mortgage interest on owner-occupied residences and the deduction for property taxes on owner-occupied residences. Many of these tax expenditures are seen as targets to be reduced or eliminated. Congress may want to consider whether the benefits of a particular tax expenditure exceed the costs of that tax expenditure. Arguably, the current tax reform debate deals with broadening the individual and corporate income tax bases and lowering marginal tax rates.

New Tax

Revenue from a new tax would allow the retention of more tax expenditures and lower reductions in other tax expenditures. Furthermore, revenue from a new tax could finance a larger reduction in marginal income tax rates and permit a smaller reduction in federal spending. Broad categories have received the most attention: consumption and environmental taxes.

Broad-Based Consumption Tax

In recent Congresses, three major types of broad-based consumption taxes have been included in congressional tax proposals: the value-added tax (VAT), the retail sales tax, and the flat tax. These possible broad-based consumption taxes have the potential of a robust revenue yield.

Value-Added Tax

A value-added tax is a tax on the value that a firm adds to a product at each stage of production. The value the firm adds is the difference between a firm's sales and a firm's purchases of inputs from other firms. The VAT is collected by each firm at every stage of production.

There are three alternative methods of calculating VAT: the credit method, the subtraction method, and the addition method. Under the credit method, the firm calculates the VAT to be remitted to the government by a two-step process. First, the firm multiplies its taxable sales by the tax rate to calculate VAT collected on sales. Second, the firm credits VAT paid on inputs against VAT collected on sales and remits this difference to the government. The firm calculates its VAT liability before setting its prices to fully shift the VAT to the buyer. Under the credit-invoice method, a type of credit method, the firm is required to show VAT separately on all sales invoices and to calculate the VAT credit on inputs by adding all VAT shown on purchase invoices.

Under the subtraction method, the firm calculates its value added by subtracting its cost of taxed inputs from its sales. Next, the firm determines its VAT liability by multiplying its value added by the VAT rate. Under the addition method, the firm calculates its value added by adding all payments for untaxed inputs (e.g., wages and profits). Next, the firm multiplies its value added by the VAT rate to calculate VAT to be remitted to the government.

All developed nations, except Japan, use the credit-invoice method. Japan uses the subtraction method.

Retail Sales Tax

A retail sales tax is a consumption tax levied only at a single stage of production, the retail stage. The retailer collects a specific percentage markup in the retail price of a good or service, which is then remitted to the government.[8] As of February 1, 2010, the Tax Foundation reports that 45 states had retail sales taxes.[9]

Flat Tax

A flat tax could be levied based on the proposal formulated by Robert E. Hall and Alvin Rabushka of the Hoover Institution.[10] Their proposal would have two components: a wage tax and a cash-flow tax on businesses. (A wage tax is a tax only on salaries and wages: a cash-flow tax is generally a tax on gross receipts minus all outlays.) It is essentially a modified VAT, with wages and pensions subtracted from the VAT base and taxed at the individual level. Under a standard VAT, a firm would not subtract its wage and pension contributions when calculating its tax base. Under the flat tax, some wage income would not be included in the tax base because of exemptions. Under a standard VAT, all wage income would be included in the tax base.

Environmental Tax

Environmental taxes have been proposed to reduce pollution and raise revenue. The most frequently discussed energy tax is a *carbon tax* that would be levied on the volume of carbon emitted. This tax is frequently recommended by economists, but the Obama Administration is attempting to implement a cap and trade system. Another alternative energy tax would be higher *gasoline taxes.*

Framework of Evaluation

In evaluating any change in tax policy, the prevailing framework is to analyze the tax policy for equity, efficiency, and simplicity. Tradeoffs may exist between these three objectives. For example, if greater income equality is desired, this may conflict with the goal of economic efficiency.

Equity

Economic theory maintains that it is not possible to make interpersonal comparisons of utility. Hence, whether a change in the distribution of income, with gainers and losers, is an improvement in the national welfare is a value judgment. The effects on different groups, however, can be measured and debated. Thus, the following questions can be examined.

How will different income groups be affected annually and over their lifetimes? Will taxpayers in similar circumstances pay approximately the same amount of taxes? What will be the effect on taxpayers in different age groups? Will there be distributional effects by region of the country? How will minority groups be affected? What will be the tax incidence on families versus single taxpayers?

Efficiency

Tax policy should promote economic efficiency; that is, a tax change should be as neutral as possible by minimizing economic distortions.[11] Low marginal tax rates tend to lessen distortions.

Many efficiency questions concern household decisions. What will be the effect of a tax change on households decisions to save versus consume? Will households' choices of leisure versus work be affected? Will household decisions about the composition of goods and services consumed be affected?

Other efficiency questions concern firms' decisions. What will be the effect on firms' decisions concerning the method of financing (debt or equity), choice among inputs, type of business organization (corporation, partnership, of sole proprietorship), and composition of output?

Simplicity

The greater the simplicity of the tax system, the lower will be the administrative and compliance costs. Thus, tax policy should eliminate any unnecessary complexity and promote transparency. Numerous questions concerning simplicity arise; among them are the following: How will a tax change affect federal administrative costs? Will the administrative costs of state and local governments change? How will compliance costs of households be affected? Will business compliance costs change?

OTHER TAX REFORM ISSUES

Alternative Minimum Tax for Individuals

In 1969, Congress enacted the individual alternative minimum tax (AMT) to make sure that everyone paid at least a minimum of income taxes and still preserve the economic and social incentives in the tax code. The combined effects of inflation and the legislative reductions in the regular income tax have expanded the number of taxpayers subject to the AMT. Consequently, Congress has passed temporary increases in the basic exemption for the AMT to limit the number of taxpayers subject to the AMT. Most recently, an AMT patch for 2010 and 2011 was included in the *Tax Relief, Unemployment Insurance Authorization, and Job Creation Act of 2010*, which became P.L. 111-312 on December 17, 2010. Some proponents of tax reform argue that the AMT should be repealed or a permanent patch should be passed, but either reform would require a major increase in taxes to offset the large revenue loss.[12]

Business Taxation

Federal taxes on business income have differential effects.[13] For example, non-corporate income is taxed less than corporate income, debt financing is an expense but equity financing is not, and depreciation rules favor machines and equipment over structures and inventory. These differential effects distort investment decisions, lessen economic efficiency, and lower economic welfare. Several options have been proposed to reform federal business taxation.[14]

First, comprehensive taxation of corporate income and lower tax rates would eliminate or reduce most major distortions. In the 112th Congress, the concept of lowering the marginal corporate income tax rate and broadening the corporate income tax base has been advocated by some members of Congress.

Second, corporate tax integration would eliminate the double taxation of corporate income by altering the general system of taxing corporate-source income. Integration could apply to both retained earnings and dividends and thus all corporate profits ("full integration"), or the treatment only of earnings that are distributed ("partial integration").

Third, a broad-based consumption tax could be levied that would replace individual and corporate income taxes.

International Taxation

The rapid growth of the foreign trade sector in the U.S. economy and the expansion of international flows of capital have increased the importance of appropriate U.S. international tax practices.[15] The two alternative principles on which countries can base their international tax systems are residence and territory.

Under a residence system, a country taxes its own residents (or domestically chartered "resident" corporations) on their worldwide income, regardless of its geographic source. Under a territorial system, a country taxes only income that is earned within its own borders. Currently, the United States has a hybrid system with elements of both a residence system and a territorial system. The United States taxes both income of foreign firms earned within its borders as well as the worldwide income of its U.S.-chartered firms. U.S. taxes, however, do not apply to the foreign income of U.S.-owned corporations chartered abroad. A U.S. firm can indefinitely defer U.S. tax on its foreign income if it conducts its foreign operations through a foreign-chartered subsidiary corporation; U.S. taxes do not apply as long as the foreign subsidiary's income is reinvested overseas. With some exceptions, U.S. taxes apply only when the income is remitted to the U.S.-resident parent as dividends or other intra-firm payments. While the United States taxes worldwide income on either a current or deferred basis, it also allows a foreign tax credit for foreign taxes paid on a dollar-for-dollar basis against U.S. taxes in order to avoid the double-taxation of income.[16]

The current system is complex and difficult to administer. Furthermore, critics argue that the current system is not sufficiently neutral, which results in economic inefficiency. The system provides a tax incentive to invest in countries with low tax rates and a disincentive to invest in countries with high tax rates. Proposals to reform the U.S. international tax system include the replacement of the current hybrid system with either a territorial tax system or a residence-based system.[17]

LEGISLATIVE OUTLOOK FOR THE 112TH CONGRESS

In the 111th Congress, numerous bills were introduced to reform the tax system. Two of those bills may be particularly relevant to the debate over tax reform in the 112th Congress. Representative Paul D. Ryan's proposal has received widespread interest because it is seen as a comprehensive plan to address America's long-term fiscal issues. Representative Ryan is chair of the House Budget Committee for the 112th Congress and served as a member of the National Commission on Fiscal Responsibility and Reform.

Senator Ron Wyden's proposal has also been widely discussed. His proposal would broaden the tax base and lower marginal tax rates. The co-chairs of the Commission (Erskine Bowles and former Senator Alan Simpson) issued a draft document in November 2010. Their comprehensive tax reform option 2 was a "Wyden-Gregg Style Reform."[18] This option was not included in the final Commission report.

Representative Paul D. Ryan's Proposal'

H.R. 4529 (111th Congress). The Roadmap for America's Future Act of 2010 was introduced January 1, 2010, and referred to the House Committee on Ways and Means, House Budget Committee, and four other committees. This bill is a comprehensive plan to address America's long-term economic and fiscal issues. Major components of the plan include health care reform, Medicare/Medicaid reform, Social Security reform, tax reform, job training reforms, and budget process reforms. Tax reform includes the elimination of the alternative minimum tax, a choice between the current income tax and a simplified income tax, the elimination of the estate and gift taxes, and the replacement of the corporate income tax with a value-added tax.[19]

The simplified income tax would have a broad base and two marginal tax rates (10% and 25%). A tax rate of 10% would apply to adjusted gross income up to $100,000 for joint filers, and $50,000 for single filers. A tax rate of 25% would apply to taxable income above $100,000 for joint filers and $50,000 for single filers. Under the simplified income tax system, the standard deduction would be $25,000 for joint filers and $12,500 for single filers, and the personal exemption would be $3,500. Thus, for a family of four, the first $39,000 of income would not be taxable.[20] Interest, dividends, and capital gains would not be taxed.

The current corporate income tax would be replaced with a subtraction-method value-added tax referred to as a Business Consumption Tax (BCT). The BCT would be levied at a rate of 8.5% and have a broad base. Temporary "transition relief" provisions would be included in order to facilitate the change from the corporate income tax.

Senator Ron Wyden's Proposal

S. 3018 (111th Congress). The Bipartisan Tax Fairness and Simplification Act of 2010 was introduced on February 23, 2010, and referred to the Senate Finance Committee. This proposal would reform the current income tax base rather than changing to a consumption base. This bill has three stated purposes: (1) to make the federal individual income tax system simpler, fairer, and more transparent; (2) to make the federal corporate income tax rate a flat 24%, repeal the corporate alternative minimum tax, and eliminate special tax preferences that favor particular types of businesses or activities; and (3) to partially offset the federal budget deficit through the increased fiscal responsibility resulting from these reforms.

The progressive individual income tax would have three rates: 15%, 25%, and 35%. The individual alternative minimum tax would be eliminated. The standard deduction would almost triple. While most deductions would be eliminated, the bill would include deductions for mortgage interest and charitable contributions. The bill would permanently extend the enhancements of the child tax credit, the earned income tax credit, and the dependent care credit.

The bill would consolidate the three existing types of IRAs into a new retirement savings account, and a new lifetime savings account. A married couple would be able to contribute up to $14,000 per year to tax-favored retirement and savings accounts. The corporate tax rate would be 24% of taxable income. The corporate tax base would be broadened by the elimination of numerous tax credits, deductions, and exclusions from income. The growth of small businesses would be encouraged by allowing businesses with gross annual receipts of up to $1 million to permanently expense all equipment and inventory costs in a single year. The bill includes numerous provisions to improve tax compliance.

End Notes

[1] Senate Committee on the Budget, Tax Expenditures: Compendium of Background Material on Individual Provisions, Washington: U.S. Govt. Print. Off., December 2008, p. 2.

[2] The National Commission on Fiscal Responsibility and Reform, The Moment of Truth, December 2010, 65 p.

[3] Ibid., p. 33.

[4] The Debt Reduction Task Force, Bipartisan Policy Center, Restoring America's Future, November 17, 2010, 138 p.

[5] Some of these proposed tax changes are examined in CRS reports.

[6] Citations of these CRS reports are shown in footnotes in the sections covering these other categories of tax reform.

[7] For an analysis of tax expenditures, see CRS Report RL34622, Tax Expenditures and the Federal Budget, by Thomas L. Hungerford.

[8] For a contrast between the VAT and the national sales tax, see CRS Report RL33438, A Value-Added Tax Contrasted With a National Sales Tax, by James M. Bickley.

[9] State Sales, Gasoline, Cigarette, and Alcohol Tax Rates by State, 2000-2010, Tax Foundation. Available at http://www.taxfoundation.org, visited January 12, 2011.

[10] For a comprehensive analysis of the flat tax, see CRS Report 98-529, Flat Tax: An Overview of the Hall-Rabushka Proposal, by James M. Bickley.

[11] The loss in economic efficiency due to a tax is referred to by economists as the deadweight loss or excess burden of the tax.

[12] For an examination of the alternative minimum tax for individuals, see CRS Report RL30149, The Alternative Minimum Tax for Individuals, by Steven Maguire.

[13] For an overview of the reform of federal business taxation, see CRS Report RL33171, Federal Business Taxation: The Current System, Its Effects, and Options for Reform, by Donald J. Marples. For an overview of corporate tax reform issues, see CRS Report RL34229, Corporate Tax Reform: Issues for Congress, by Jane G. Gravelle and Thomas L. Hungerford.

[14] For a comprehensive analysis of these options, see CRS Report RL33171, Federal Business Taxation: The Current System, Its Effects, and Options for Reform, by Donald J. Marples.

[15] This section of this report summarizes some basic concepts in CRS Report RL34115, Reform of U.S. International Taxation: Alternatives, by Jane G. Gravelle. Some excerpts are stated from this report.

[16] Ibid., p. 2.

[17] Ibid., pp. 12-16.

[18] Co-Chairs' Proposal, Draft Document, November 2010, p. 27.

[19] For a comprehensive explanation of this proposed legislation, see A Roadmap for America's Future, available at http://www.roadmap.republicans.budget.house.gov/.

[20] A family of four assumes a married couple plus two dependent children.

In: Federal Taxation
Editor: Jaclyn N. Prichard
ISBN: 978-1-61324-102-8

Chapter 3

FEDERAL BUSINESS TAXATION: THE CURRENT SYSTEM, ITS EFFECTS, AND OPTIONS FOR REFORM*

Donald J. Marples

SUMMARY

A foundation of the broad tax revisions implemented 24 years ago by the Tax Reform Act of 1986 was tax "neutrality"—the idea that economic efficiency and economic welfare are promoted if the distorting impact of taxes on business and other economic decisions is minimized. Based on this principle, the 1986 act broadened the tax base and reduced statutory tax rates set forth by the tax code. In time, however, the underlying thrust of tax policy has changed. Rather than neutrality and efficiency, recent business tax legislation has been guided more by a concern for promoting investment and capital formation, and by attention to the perceived impact of taxes on the ability of U.S. firms to compete with foreign companies. Further, recent interest in fundamental tax reform has been partly stimulated by these same concerns for capital formation and competitiveness.

Twenty-four years after the 1986 act, business tax policy is thus potentially at a crossroads, and it is useful to take stock of where the system stands, the economic effects it is known to have, and the principal options for reform. Several data series show a similar pattern in the level of corporate

* This is an edited, reformatted and augmented version of Congressional Research Services publication RL33171, dated September 9, 2010.

taxes: corporate income taxes have generally declined over the post-World War II period. At the same time, however, significant disparities in the structure of business taxes have remained, suggesting a persistence of distortions caused by the tax system: corporate-sector investment remains heavily taxed compared to non-corporate business and owner-occupied housing; debt is favored over equity; and equipment is favored over structures.

The base of business taxation is the return to business investment; business taxes thus influence the economy through their impact on investment. In broad terms, business taxes can, at least in principle, reduce capital formation and thus impair long-term economic growth by making saving and investment less attractive. This effect, however, depends on a robust saving response to taxes, the presence of which is uncertain. Another impact is on the allocation of investment among different sectors and asset types. Here, business taxes likely distort investment decisions, reducing economic efficiency and economic welfare. In the case of equity, economic theory suggests that in the long run, the burden of business taxation is shared among all owners of capital and has a progressive effect on the tax system.

Various hypothetical alternatives exist for reforming the business tax system. One possibility is to move in the direction of the 1986 Tax Reform Act by broadening the existing tax base—that is,

by eliminating tax benefits and preferences. Another possibility—and one that is favored by many economists—is to adopt some form of tax integration that would eliminate the double taxation of corporate income. A third option is to adopt a form of consumption tax, under which new

business investment would be exempt from tax. Either corporate tax integration or a consumption tax could improve economic efficiency, but only if the design were to avoid the types of distortions present in the current system.

This report will be updated in the event of major changes in the business tax system.

INTRODUCTION

Twenty-four years ago, the broad tax revisions implemented by the Tax Reform Act of 1986 (P.L. 99-514) were based on tax "neutrality"—the idea that economic efficiency and economic welfare are promoted if the distorting impact of taxes on business and other economic decisions is minimized. To this end, the 1986 act broadened the tax base for both businesses and individuals, scaling back various narrowly-applicable tax preferences and benefits, and reduced the statutory tax rate.

In time, however, the general thrust of business-tax policy began to change, and in recent years policy has been guided more by a concern for the level of investment and capital formation, as well as the perceived impact of taxes on U.S. competitiveness. Thus, measures designed to promote tax-consistency across investments and activities have been supplanted by provisions designed to stimulate investment and assist in the ability of U.S. firms to compete with foreign companies. Cases in point are the temporary "bonus depreciation" provisions enacted in 2002 and 2003 and the broad tax deduction for domestic production included in the omnibus business-tax bill passed in 2004.[1] At the same time, there has recently been renewed congressional and public interest in broad reform of the U.S. tax system. In contrast to 1986, however, much of the recent interest in reform has centered on a shift in the tax base to consumption rather than a comprehensive measure of income—a change in focus that is based, in part, on the same concerns for capital formation and competitiveness that underlie much of recent business-tax legislation.

Twenty-four years after the 1986 act, business taxation is thus potentially at a crossroads. Will the thrust of tax policy continue to shift away from the principles of efficiency and neutrality that guided tax reform two decades in the past? If fundamental tax reform is adopted in the near future, would it include a revamped system of business taxation? If so, what would business taxation look like? Regardless of the outcome, it is useful at this point to take stock, to pause and review the current system and its effects. The charts and discussions on the following pages are intended to assist in that exercise. The report begins with a discussion of the principal economic effects of business taxation. Its concluding sections review the various theoretical principles on which fundamental reform of business taxation might be based.

BASIC STRUCTURE OF THE CURRENT SYSTEM

Businesses can take a variety of forms, ranging from large, publicly held corporations, to more closely held corporations, to partnerships (large and small), to firms that are run by only a single self-employed owner. With some exceptions, the rules for determining taxable income—for example, how to calculate depreciation and other deductions—are the same, regardless of the type of business. The particular manner in which that income is taxed, however, does vary, depending on the type of business.

Income earned by large, publicly held corporations ("C" corporations, in tax parlance) is generally subject to the corporate income tax—one of the principal structural components of the federal tax system, along with the individual income tax, the estate and gift tax, excise taxes, and social security taxes. In conceptual terms, the present U.S. corporate income tax is sometimes described as a "classical" system that applies as though corporations were entities with an existence separate from their owners, the stockholders. The tax applies to taxable corporate income, corporate profits (after deducting interest) as defined by the tax code. It applies separately and in addition to the individual income tax's applicability to shareholder's dividends and capital gains. As discussed in more detail below (see the section on the economic effects of the tax), this means that income subject to the corporate income tax is generally taxed twice— once under the corporate income tax in the hands of corporations, and once under the individual income tax when stockholders receive dividends or realize capital gains. The double taxation does not occur, however, in the case of corporate income generated by debt-financed investment, since the return to such investment is paid to creditors as interest and is tax-deductible. Double taxation also does not apply in the case of income paid to tax-exempt stockholders—for example, pension funds.

Income earned by relatively closely held corporations—termed "S corporations" by the tax code—is not subject to the corporate income tax and so also is not taxed twice. Instead, an S corporation's income is "passed through" to the firm's stockholders and taxed to them under the individual income tax, regardless of whether the income is actually distributed. To qualify as an S corporation, a firm can have no more than 100 shareholders and must meet certain other requirements.

As with S-corporation profits, partnership taxable income is not subject to an entity-level tax such as the corporate income tax. Instead, each partner is taxed under the individual income tax on his or her share of the partnership's profit.[2] Individual income taxes also apply to business income earned by self-employed persons who operate sole proprietorships. As with partnerships and S corporations, no separate tax is applied at the entity (i.e., business) level.

According to estimates by the Congressional Budget Office, 62% of tangible business assets are owned by C corporations; the remainder (38%) is owned by other business entities (i.e., partnerships, sole proprietorships, and S corporations).[3]

As noted above, rules for determining taxable income are generally the same, regardless of the form of business organization.[4] The base of federal business income taxes is generally profits, net of interest payments. Profits, in turn, are gross receipts—for example, sales—minus deductible costs. Important categories of deductible costs include interest payments, wages, purchased materials and other inputs, and a depreciation allowance for the decline in value of tangible capital. Importantly, the tax code's definition of these elements frequently differs from how an economist or accountant might define them. For example, the tax code may fully or partly exempt certain types of income from inclusion in taxable income—a specific example is the partial deduction the tax code permits for income from domestic production activities. Or, the tax code may require the recognition of income at a different point in time than when economic theory indicates it is actually earned or permit a deduction to be claimed at a different time from when the cost is actually incurred. Regardless of the underlying provision, instances where taxable income differs from economic income can provide either a tax benefit or tax penalty and (as described more fully below) influence how the economy's capital resources are allocated.

U.S. firms increasingly participate in international markets, and so an overview of the U.S. structure would be incomplete without including its international dimension. In the international context, the U.S. applies what is sometimes termed a "residence" based tax system, but with important exceptions. The United States generally applies its corporate income to the worldwide income of corporations chartered in (i.e., "resident" in) the United States. At the same time, however, U.S. firms can generally indefinitely postpone (defer) U.S. tax on foreign-source income as long as the income is earned by foreign-chartered subsidiary corporations and reinvested abroad. To alleviate double taxation, the United States permits its taxpayers to credit foreign taxes they pay against U.S. taxes they would otherwise owe, subject to the limitation that foreign taxes can only be credited against U.S. foreign- (and not U.S.-) source income Foreign businesses in the United States are generally subject to U.S. business taxes on their U.S.- source income. If a foreign firm operates in the United States through a U.S.-chartered subsidiary corporation, the subsidiary is generally subject to U.S. tax in its role as a resident U.S. corporation; like other U.S.-chartered corporations, it is subject to U.S. tax on its worldwide income, regardless of the nationality of its owner(s). If, on the other hand, the foreign firm operates in the United States through a branch of the foreign-chartered parent corporation, the foreign firm is subject to U.S. tax on its income from U.S., but not foreign, sources; the United States taxes foreign persons and corporations on their income from the active conduct of a U.S. trade or business. (The economic effects of international aspects of the federal tax system are discussed below.)

Another structural component of the system is the alternative minimum tax (AMT). The tax code provides both a corporate AMT and an individual AMT; a business may be subject to either, depending on whether it pays the corporate income tax or is taxed under the individual income tax as a sole proprietorship or passthrough entity. Both AMTs essentially require a taxpayer to pay either the regular tax or the AMT, whichever is higher. The two liabilities will ordinarily differ for a business because they are computed differently. The AMT is imposed at a lower statutory rate than the regular tax, and the base of the AMT is more inclusive than that of the regular tax, permitting fewer omissions and tax benefits. The purpose of the AMT is to ensure that few truly profitable corporations escape paying at least some tax.

The importance of the AMT in the structure is difficult to quantify. Recent data on the share of corporate investment subject to the tax are not available. The numbers that are available show that prior to 1999, the AMT was important: in 1998, more than one-quarter of corporate assets were held by firms paying the AMT, and within the manufacturing sector over one-half of firms were AMT firms. Beginning in 1999, however, new, more generous AMT depreciation rules likely reduced the portion of investment affected by the AMT.

Level of Corporate Taxes, Past and Present

The level of corporate tax receipts has fluctuated over time. This review of the data focuses primarily on the corporate income tax; there are a variety of ways to gauge its size. First, the general importance of the tax in terms of any economic effects it has can be assessed by looking at the level of the tax compared to the size of the economy—that is, by assessing corporate tax revenue as a percent of gross domestic product (GDP). Figure 1, below, presents such data for fiscal years 1934 to 2009, thus showing the position of corporate revenues from well before World War II to the latest year available. Clearly, the chart shows that corporate tax revenues have declined from their peak during World War II (7% in FY1945) and from another peak that coincided with the Korean War (6.1% in FY1952). The chart also shows that they have declined from what might be termed an intermediate level of between 2% and 4% in the 1960s and 1970s to a level between 1% and 2% in recent years, but with an "uptick" beginning in 2005 before falling dramatically in 2009.

While corporate taxes have declined as a percentage of GDP, Figure 2, below, shows that corporate income-tax revenue likewise declined as a share of total federal revenue, and in roughly the same pattern. Corporate tax revenue's share of total federal revenue declined from a peak of 40% during World War II (FY1943), and a somewhat lower peak of 32% during the Korean War (FY1952), to levels of slightly above and below 10% after the late 1980s. Again, there was a surge beginning in 2005 before falling dramatically in 2009.

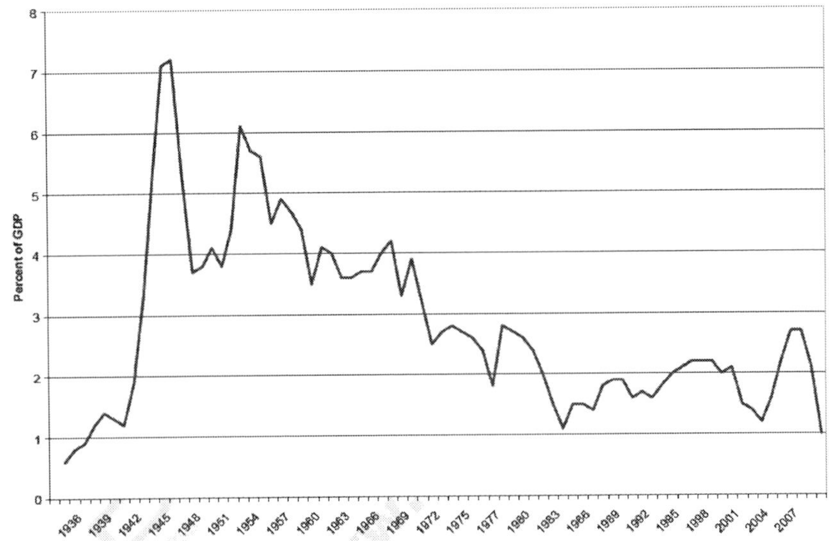

Source: U.S. Office of Management and Budget, *Historical Tables: Budget of the United States, Fiscal Year 2011* (Washington: GPO, 2010).

Figure 1. Corporate Taxes as a Percentage of GDP, FY1934-FY2009.

Source: U.S. Office of Management and Budget, *Historical Tables: Budget of the United States, Fiscal Year 2011* (Washington: GPO, 2010).

Figure 2. Corporate Tax Revenue as a Percentage of Total Federal Tax Revenue, FY1934-FY2009.

Source: CRS Report RL30469, Average Effective Corporate Tax Rates: 1959 to 2005, by Steven Maguire.

Figure 3. Average Effective Corporate Tax Rates: Federal Corporate Taxes as a Percentage of Corporate Profits, FY1959-FY2005.

These broad measures of corporate taxes are useful as rough indicators of how the level of corporate taxes in the economy has changed, but lack precision in showing the burden of corporate taxes and the causes of the taxes' fluctuations. For example, a decline in the share of national income comprising corporate profits is partly responsible for the reductions shown in Figures 1 and 2. Figure 3 corrects for this with a series that holds profits constant. It shows average effective corporate tax rates (AETRs), which are the ratio of federal corporate income taxes to before-tax corporate profits. According to the AETRs, the aggregate burden of corporate taxes steadily declined during the 1960s and 1970s, reaching a low of about 20% of corporate profits during the early 1980s before rising to a plateau of around 25% that has generally prevailed from 1986 to the present. The anomalous year in the last two decades was 2000, which registered a spike in the AETR to 34%.

Since AETRs hold the level of corporate profits constant, a principal determinant of variations in the rates is legislated changes, and several can be linked to the fluctuations in the AETRS. At least three factors are likely responsible for the decline in rates during the 1960s, 1970s, and early 1980s. First, during the 1970s and 1980s, several reductions in the statutory corporate tax rate that applies to taxable income were enacted. Second, while taxable corporate profits were artificially inflated during the 1970s by a rising price level, firms were also permitted to claim investment tax credits. Third, the Economic Recovery Tax Act of 1981 provided accelerated depreciation deductions, which likely played a prominent role in the sharp drop in tax rates in the early 1980s. Following the reduction, rates increased again in the mid-1980s. Part of the increase was likely due to timing results from the 1981 act, but the Tax Reform Act of 1986 was also likely responsible for part of the increase. The act reduced statutory tax rates, but also repealed the investment credit and scaled back depreciation allowances.

AETRs have their own shortcoming as a gauge of the corporate tax burden. They provide only one-year snapshots of a firm's tax burden, while according to economic theory, taxes impose a burden on capital income by reducing the expected rate of return over the life of new investment. For example, the tax burden on an investment consists not only of taxes paid in its first year, but also those paid in, say, the fifth year of its life. In addition, because of discounting, the tax burden on investment depends partly on how taxes are distributed over an investment's life; a given amount of taxes matters more to a firm the sooner it is paid. The same is true of deductions, but in reverse; a given deduction is more valuable the sooner it is claimed.

"Marginal" effective tax rates (METRs) take these factors into account, measuring the impact of taxes over a representative investment's entire lifetime as well as the timing of payments and deductions. Unlike AETRs, METRs can thus accurately register the impact of provisions such as accelerated depreciation, whose value depends crucially on timing. METRs also take into account the interaction of inflation and tax rules, statutory tax rates, and investment subsidies such as the investment tax credit. In general, a marginal effective tax rate is the difference between the pretax and after-tax return on prospective investment, divided by the pre-tax return.[5]

Figure 4, below, presents a set of METRs for the period 1953 through 2005. The top line in the figure shows METRs for corporate investment. The second line is rates for non-corporate business and moves in tandem with corporate rates, but at a lower level. (The third line is the METR for the remaining broad category of capital investment: owner-occupied housing.) The series shows a decline in rates from the early 1950s to the mid-1960s—the result of accelerated depreciation, introduction of an investment tax credit, and reduced statutory tax rates. Rates then rose in the late 1960s and varied during the 1970s, a consequence of repeal and reintroduction of the investment tax credit as well as inflation. Rates declined sharply in 1981, reflecting the Economic Recovery Tax Act's accelerated depreciation provisions. METRs then remained relatively stable until 2001 to 2003, when reductions in shareholder-level taxes (including reduced tax rates on capital gains and dividends) as well as bonus depreciation caused a reduction in effective rates. Rates picked up again in 2005, with the expiration of bonus depreciation.[6]

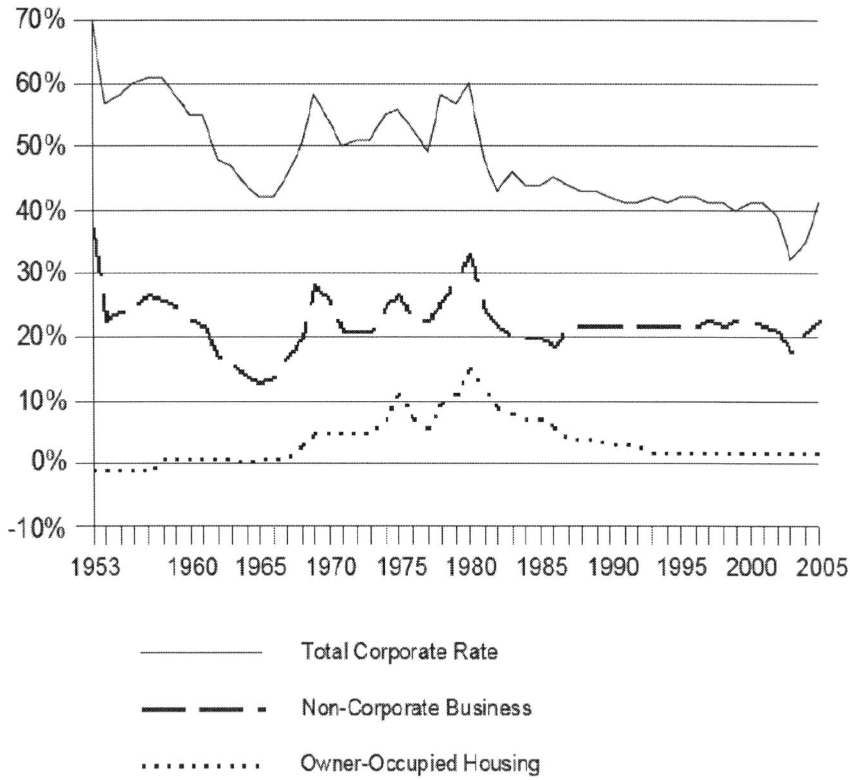

Source: CRS Report RS21706, Historical Effective Marginal Tax Rates on Capital Income, by Jane G. Gravelle.

Figure 4. Marginal Effective Tax Rates on Corporate and Other Investment, FY1953-FY2005.

The preceding charts show four different measures of corporate taxes: taxes as a share of GDP, corporate tax revenues as a percentage of federal revenue, average effective corporate tax rates, and marginal effective tax rates. Each series shows the same general pattern in the period after World War II: a general decline in the level of corporate taxes. But before accepting this broad pattern as the conclusion of this look at corporate tax data, note the relative position of the three lines in Figure 4, denoting METRs for corporate investment, for non-corporate business, and for owner-occupied housing. In contrast to the general direction of each set of METRs—they have all declined, showing a decline in capital taxes in general—their relative position has remained the same. And importantly, it is the relative tax treatment of investment that affects the allocation of investment among different uses, and differences in the treatment of different investments that distort the allocation of capital. Thus, to the conclusion that business taxes have generally declined in the post-World War II period, there is an additional important result: corporate investment remains relatively heavily taxed compared to non-corporate business and (especially) owner-occupied housing.[7] The report's next section explores the implications of this result by discussing the economic effects of business taxes.

ECONOMIC EFFECTS OF BUSINESS TAXES

The base of the corporate income tax and of business taxes in general is income from capital investment. It is thus not surprising that business taxes exert their most direct effects through their impact on the return to new investment. By reducing the return to capital investment, business taxes—at least in principle—can affect the economy's commitment of resources to capital formation in general, although this effect may be muted. Business taxes can also affect the allocation of investment funds among different sectors, as suggested at the end of the preceding section. And while businesses are not people, the burden of business taxes is ultimately borne by individuals; business taxes thus have an impact on the fairness of the tax system.

Business Taxes and Capital Formation

Because they apply to the return on investment, business taxes can potentially reduce the economy's overall level of investment and its stock of capital. There are indeed some who advocate cutting business taxes as a means of boosting capital formation: according to economic theory, an increase in the capital stock boosts long run growth, which, in turn, increases living standards and per capita income in the future.[8]

Yet business taxes do not necessarily have a pronounced effect on the aggregate level of capital in the economy. A key element is the economy's supply of saving, and there are indications that individual savers may not respond robustly to tax cuts by increasing their saving. Note first, however, that business taxes do likely have an impact on firms' investment demand. Taxes on business profits increase the rate of return a given asset must earn, before taxes, in order to generate the rate of return required to attract funds from savers. A tax on business investment thus encourages firms to forgo a range of less profitable investments they might otherwise undertake. And indeed, as described below, uneven application of business taxes results in less investment in heavily taxed areas and more investment in lightly taxed projects.

But investment demand is just one side of the market for capital; the other side is household saving. And if individual saving is unresponsive to changes in the after-tax rate of return, then changes in investment demand will have little impact on the overall stock of capital: boosts in demand will principally serve to increase the economy's real interest rate. For example, provision of a tax credit for businesses to undertake investment may indeed boost business demand for the particular type of investment in question, and firms may boost the rate of return they are willing to pay savers for each quantity of investment. But unless savers are willing to increase the quantity of funds they supply in response to the higher return, there will be no increase in the capital stock.

Economic theory provides no unambiguous answer on how saving responds to its rate of return, after taxes, and is subject to countervailing effects. In isolation, a tax on investment income—that is, on saving—reduces the price of current consumption compared to future consumption, and may thus reduce saving. On the other hand, a tax on saving increases the amount of saving an individual must undertake before taxes in order to achieve a particular dollar amount, after taxes, and may thus increase saving. The answer to the question therefore depends on the empirical evidence. And while there have been numerous econometric studies of saving, their results differ.[9] This has led some to suggest that instead of providing tax incentives for saving and investment, a more certain approach to boosting aggregate national saving would be reducing government dissaving by reducing the government's budget deficit.[10]

Business Taxes and Economic Efficiency

Not only does the amount of capital matter for economic performance, but so too does how that capital is employed. And while business taxes likely have little impact on long-run growth and capital formation, they do affect the allocation of investment among different uses and thus affect economic efficiency. Because taxes affect investment demand, they distort the allocation of investment where they apply unevenly, channeling funds to tax-favored assets and away from more heavily taxed assets. The results for economic efficiency follow: economic theory indicates that undistorted market prices and investment returns generally allocate resources to their most productive use so that capital and other resources produce the mix of output that consumers value most, and economic welfare is maximized. To the extent business taxes distort the allocation of resources, they reduce economic welfare.

One prominent distortion posed by the U.S. tax system results from the double-taxation of corporate-source equity income—its taxation under both the corporate income tax and the individual income tax. As a result, investment is channeled away from the corporate sector into less heavily taxed areas such as owner-occupied housing and non-corporate business (see the effective tax rates in Figure 4, above). A second distortion posed by the corporate income tax is its favoring of debt over equity in the financing of investment. The return to debt-financed investment consists of corporate interest payments to creditors; the return to equity consists of dividends and capital gains. Since interest is tax-deductible at the corporate level but dividends and capital gains are not, firms are encouraged to use higher levels of debt than they otherwise would, increasing the risk of bankruptcy to an inefficiently high level.

Different types of business assets are also taxed at different rates, encouraging firms to invest more heavily in favored assets than they otherwise would. The depreciation allowances that apply to machines and equipment are relatively generous compared to depreciation allowances for structures and capital-recovery methods for inventory, leading to a relatively light tax burden for machines and equipment. Thus, firms' asset choices are distorted, encouraging more investment in machines and equipment and less in structures and inventory than is economically efficient.

Prior to the Tax Reform of Act of 1986, the differential tax burdens among assets were substantial—a consequence of a relatively high statutory tax rate, relatively high inflation, uneven depreciation rules, and the availability of an investment tax credit for equipment, but not other assets. The 1986 act altered depreciation rules, repealed the investment credit, and reduced the statutory corporate tax rate, thereby greatly diminishing inter-asset distortions. In recent years, however, both legislation and economic developments have reintroduced differential tax burdens, though not to the extent existent before 1986. Legislative changes included introduction of less-favorable depreciation for structures, bonus depreciation for equipment, and an increased statutory tax rate.[11]

As noted above, the corporate income tax distorts corporate financial policy, favoring debt finance. Another distortion of corporate financial policy results from individual rather than corporate income taxation, and the preferential treatment of capital gains. Specifically, since capital gains are not subject to individual income taxes until a stockholder sells stock and the gains are realized, taxes favor the corporate retention of earnings—which increases the value of corporate stock—over payout of dividends. Recent legislation has reduced the statutory tax rate on dividends to the same rate applicable to realized capital gains, which has reduced the difference between the effective tax rates of retentions and payouts. Nonetheless, a difference remains because capital gains are not taxed until realized while dividends are taxed on a current basis.

Business Taxes and Equity

Corporations are not people: they are economic entities (firms) taking a particular legal form (incorporation). Thus, corporations cannot bear the burden of the corporate income tax in any real sense: it ultimately is borne by individuals. In the short run—that is, before economic actors have had a chance to adjust to the tax—the tax is thought to be borne by corporate stockholders

The long-run burden of the tax is more uncertain. The standard and most resilient economic model of the corporate income tax is that developed by Arnold Harberger in 1962.[12] While a number of challenges have been made to the model since its inception, its results have generally proved resilient.[13] The model concludes that if capital investment funds and labor are free to flow from one economic sector (e.g., the corporate sector) to another (and given certain other conditions), then wages, prices, rates of return, and the allocation of capital and labor adjust, in the long run, to the corporate income tax. Given the ability of economic actors to adjust, the burden of the corporate income tax spreads beyond corporate shareholders' sector to all owners of capital, including owners of corporate debt, non-corporate business, and owner-occupied housing.

This picture of the long-run burden of the corporate tax has implications for the vertical equity of the tax system—that is, its distribution across income classes. Because capital ownership is greater at upper-income levels, the corporate income tax is itself progressive and makes the overall tax system more progressive than it would otherwise be.

Business Taxes and Compctitiveness

A widely cited reason for reforming U.S. business taxation is to improve U.S. "competitiveness," where competitiveness is usually a loosely defined term generally meaning the ability of U.S. firms to compete with foreign businesses, whether by means of export sales or sales by U.S. firms who have invested abroad. Yet there are few areas in which economic theory and popular beliefs diverge more widely than in international economics and notions of "competitiveness." Given the prominence of competitiveness in the public debate, it is thus useful to examine the international dimension of business taxes' effects in some detail.

Taxes and Trade

Contrary to popular arguments that are sometimes made, economic theory indicates that business taxes do not affect the nation's balance of trade—that is, the imposition of federal taxes on business profits does not increase the U.S. trade deficit by reducing U.S. exports or increasing imports. This conclusion may counter intuition at first—surely the imposition of a tax on the profits of a U.S. exporting firm will reduce its sales to foreigners and thus reduce aggregate U.S. exports. But economic theory's rebuttal is equally intuitive: just as an individual cannot consume more than he earns unless he borrows, a country cannot use more than it produces—cannot import more than it exports—unless it borrows to finance the difference by importing foreign investment. Thus, a country can only increase its trade deficit if it imports some additional amount of foreign investment; a country's net exports only increase if its net overseas investment also increases.[14]

In slightly more technical terms, a country's balance of trade (its balance on goods and services) mirrors its balance on capital account; the balance of trade changes only if the balance on capital account likewise changes. This relationship is an identity that holds whether or not the international economy is in equilibrium. The particular economic mechanism that enforces the identity under the current regime of flexible exchange rates is exchange rate adjustments. Even if a change in an exogenous variable (e.g., taxes) would otherwise increase net exports, exchange rates adjust to offset any change that would otherwise occur.

The implication of this analysis is that business taxes alter the balance of trade only if they also alter net flows of international investment (the balance on capital account). As an illustration, the United States repealed a tax benefit for exporting known as the extraterritorial income (ETI) benefit in 2004. Some observers feared that ETI's repeal would harm U.S. competitiveness. Economic theory, however, suggests that ETI's repeal would have no direct impact on the balance of trade. While some reduction of exports may initially occur, that reduction will stimulate a fall in the price of the dollar in currency markets below what would otherwise occur. The dollar's depreciation will mitigate the initial decline in exports and will also reduce imports. There will be no change in the trade balance (exports minus imports).

While business taxes do not affect the trade balance, they can affect the composition of its trade. This outcome follows from one of the foundations of economic trade theory—the theory of comparative advantage. According to this theory, the composition of a country's exports and imports is determined not by how the costs of domestic goods compare to those of foreign goods, but rather by how the costs of domestic goods compare to each other. Under comparative advantage, a country exports what it can produce at lowest cost. The particular composition of its exports and imports thus depends on the particular pattern of costs across all of its products and potential products. Business taxes can alter this pattern of costs and thus alter the content of trade. For example, if taxes apply heavily to one item and fall lightly on another, they encourage the import of the first product and the export of the second.

But if business taxes cannot increase net exports and can only change the pattern of trade, this is not necessarily bad news. Standard economic trade theory indicates that countries gain economic welfare by exchanging exports for imports; the exchange enables each trading country to specialize in producing what it produces most efficiently while not sacrificing its use of the higher-cost goods that it imports. In short, a country's economic welfare is not enhanced by the mere act of exporting; it is the ability to exchange exports for imports that makes a country better off (that produces "gains from trade," in economic parlance).

Taxes can reduce economic welfare through their impact on trade in a number of ways. One is a reduction in economic efficiency similar to those described in preceding section, but translated to the international economy. If taxes apply unevenly, they may distort the pattern of costs within the economy and distort the composition of trade, thus encouraging a country to specialize in activities at which it is relatively inefficient. A second way taxes can reduce a country's economic welfare is to worsen its "terms of trade," or the quantity (in real terms) of exports it must give up to obtain a given quantity of imports. For example, if part of the benefit of an export subsidy (e.g., ETI) is passed on to foreign consumers in the form of lower prices, the subsidy worsens the subsidizing country's terms of trade; its exports are cheaper for foreign consumers. The subsidizing country's economic welfare is reduced because its own taxpayers are underwriting the price reduction for foreign consumers.

Taxes and International Business Investment

Business taxes can have a direct impact on the extent to which U.S. firms invest abroad, and also the extent to which foreign firms invest in the United States. Here, the crucial factor is how taxes (both U.S. and foreign) on an investment in a foreign location compare to taxes on an identical investment undertaken in the United States. To the extent taxes in the foreign location are lower than those on the U.S. project, taxes encourage overseas investment; to the extent U.S. taxes are low relative to taxes on the overseas investment, they encourage domestic, over foreign, investment. If taxes are the same in either location, they have no impact (are "neutral") on location choice.

According to traditional economic theory, taxes best promote economic efficiency by not distorting the location of investment; neutrality between overseas and domestic investment best promotes efficiency. But the overall impact of the U.S. system is uncertain. As described above, the United States in some situations taxes the overseas income of its firms on a current basis, while in other instances it permits an indefinite deferral of taxes on foreign-source income; foreign tax credits are provided to alleviate double taxation. The net result of this system for the relative tax burden on foreign and domestic investment is mixed; the system produces a patchwork of incentives, disincentives, and neutrality towards overseas investment that varies, depending on factors such as the level of foreign taxes applied to the investment, the legal form of the investment, and the location and nature of a firm's other foreign investments. The efficiency effect of the system is thus not clear.

BUSINESS TAXES AND TAX REFORM

The first section of this report outlined the current structure of federal business taxation—a separate tax on corporate profits imposed in addition to the individual income tax and net of interest; and taxation of unincorporated business on a current basis under the individual income tax. The report's section on business tax data indicated that while the level of business taxes has generally declined since World War II, important divergences remain in the way different types of investment are taxed. The section on economic effects indicated that these effects can impair economic efficiency, although they likely do not hinder U.S. competitiveness. With these pictures in mind, the report now turns to the principal options for reform that have been developed for business tax policy.

Comprehensive Taxation of Business Income

Since corporations are economic and legal entities and not people, the question might be raised: why impose a separate corporate income tax at all? The question is made more pointed when the detrimental efficiency effects of a separate tax on corporate income are considered—effects such as the diversion of investment away from equity investment in the corporate sector. A number of arguments, however, can be mounted in favor of a separate tax on corporate income. First, since stock ownership in particular, and ownership of capital in general, is more prevalent among upper-income individuals, the corporate income tax adds an element of progressivity to the tax system; its repeal—absent compensating changes elsewhere in the system—would be, in isolation, a regressive policy change. Second, corporate managers may be able to exercise considerable independence from stockholders in their decisions about corporate investment. To the extent this occurs, corporations do have some existence separate from their stockholders. Third, without a corporate income tax (or tax integration plan, as outlined below), retained corporate earnings would receive favorable tax treatment. And finally, even if corporations are not people and have no existence separate from their stockholders, many individual taxpayers nonetheless compare the taxes they pay with those paid by large corporations and draw conclusions about fairness from that comparison. And even if such comparisons, from an economic standpoint, are not appropriate, they do affect perceptions about the fairness of the tax system—perceptions that are important to the acceptance of the tax system by the public at large.

While the current system does tax corporations as though they were separate entities, it does not do so on a comprehensive basis. Numerous important omissions from the tax base would exist if all corporate profits were taxed on the same basis. Thus, if the validity of a separate corporate income tax is accepted, one hypothetical direction that tax reform might take is to move in the direction of a more pure version of the "classical" system of taxing corporate income—to eliminate the various omissions in the tax base and non-neutralities embedded in the current system. Setting aside the distortions that result from the existence of the corporate income tax in the first place, such a reform would likely minimize the inefficiencies and distortions that exist within the classical system. As noted at the outset of the report, such was a guiding principle of the Tax Reform Act of 1986.

How much does the current system depart from a comprehensive tax on corporate income? One considerable departure is the omission of income from debt-financed investment from the tax base—an omission that occurs when interest payments are deducted. Income generated by debt-financed investment is income from capital just as surely as is income from equity investment. Debt's omission from the tax base distorts firms' financing choices, favoring debt over equity and enticing firms to accept a higher risk of bankruptcy than is economically efficient. Nonetheless, simple elimination of interest deductibility has rarely been proposed outside of a movement away from the classical system by adoption, for example, of tax integration (discussed below).[15]

Another important determinant of the corporate tax base is depreciation. One important element of the 1986 act's reform was its evening-out of depreciation allowances across assets. The act implemented depreciation allowances that were more closely aligned with actual economic depreciation. Together with the act's repeal of the investment tax credit, the depreciation revisions reduced prior law's general preference for equipment and relatively short-lived assets over structures. Since 1986, however, a wedge has reemerged between equipment and structures, although—setting aside the temporary bonus depreciation for equipment—this has been more a consequence of changed economic conditions (reduced inflation) and a lengthening of depreciation allowances for structures than reintroduction of accelerated depreciation.[16] Nonetheless, a likely ingredient of tax reform based on comprehensive income taxation would be a realignment of depreciation allowances with economic depreciation.

Another prominent departure from comprehensive taxation is the deduction for domestic production that was enacted by the American Jobs Creation Act of 2004 (P.L. 108-357). The deduction is 9% of income from domestic production activities; it cannot be applied to income from overseas investment. Other omissions from the tax base are more narrowly targeted tax benefits—for example, the section 179 expensing allowance from equipment investment of small businesses, the tax credit for research and experimentation, and various provisions applicable to the oil and gas industry. The Joint Committee on Taxation (JCT) maintains a list of "tax expenditures" or provisions that carve out special tax treatment for particular activities, income, or investments; a relatively comprehensive list of omissions from the corporate tax base can be obtained by consulting the JCT list.[17] A tax reform that moves in the direction of comprehensive income taxation would presumably scale back items included in the list of tax expenditures.

Corporate Tax Integration

As described above in the section on the economic effects of business taxation, the current "classical" system of taxing corporate income results in a number of distortions in the allocation of investment, thus reducing economic efficiency and causing a concomitant reduction in economic welfare. For this reason, economists have long advocated some form of tax "integration"—a term that refers to eliminating double taxation of corporate income by altering the general system of taxing corporate-source income.

Integration proposals vary, but fall into two broad categories: those that apply to both retained earnings and dividends and thus all corporate profits ("full integration"), and those that change the treatment only of earnings that are distributed ("partial integration").

There are three basic approaches to full integration, which differ in whether double taxation is removed at the corporate level or at the individual level. The "shareholder allocation" method is similar to partnership taxation. The corporate income tax would be repealed, and corporate profits—whether retained or distributed—would be allocated among the firm's owners, who would pay individual income taxes on the corporate income. Thus, corporate income would be taxed once, in the hands of individuals.

A second approach is "shareholder credit" integration, under which the corporate income tax would be retained, but corporate stockholders would receive a tax credit for the corporate-level taxes paid by the paying corporation. An adjustment to the capital gains portion of the credit would be made to account for the capital gains resulting from both retained earnings (that have been subject to the corporate income tax) and other price appreciation. Under this approach, while relief would be provided at the individual level, taxes would be paid on the corporate income tax at individual income tax rates. Thus, the corporate income tax would function much like a withholding tax.

A third approach is to retain the corporate income tax, but exclude corporate-source income from individual income taxes—a relatively simple method to implement for distributed earnings, but difficult to administer for the portion of capital gains attributable to reinvested earnings. In the latter case, stockholders' basis in stock would have to be adjusted to reflect retained earnings, so as to exclude only gains attributable to retained earnings. In 1992, a U.S. Treasury report outlined a variant of this method, termed a "comprehensive business income tax" (CBIT), under which corporate-source income would not be taxed at the individual level. The corporate income tax would be retained, and interest deductions would not be permitted.

Partial integration by means of an exclusion for dividends received by stockholders would thus be relatively straightforward. Indeed, the reduced individual income tax rate that the Jobs and Growth Tax Relief Act of 2003 (JGTRRA) applied to dividend income can be viewed as a form of shareholder-level partial integration, akin to a shareholder exclusion that applies to only part of received dividends. Similarly, a shareholder-credit version of integration that would be restricted to dividends paid would be more straightforward than the full-integration version of a credit system. A partial-integration form of the shareholder credit method is the system used most frequently by European and other foreign countries that have adopted integration.

Each method of integration has its particular advantages and disadvantages. As suggested in the preceding discussion, partial integration is simpler and easier to administer than full integration; on the other hand, it does not achieve all the efficiency gains under full integration, since a part of corporate income would still be taxed twice. Also, the different plans differ in their revenue cost, with the full-integration methods generally losing more revenue than partial integration plans, and shareholder allocation methods reducing revenue more than other methods.[18]

Business Taxes under Consumption or Flat Taxes

Either tax integration or a tax based on a comprehensive measure of income would qualify as fundamental tax reform. Each would entail substantial changes to the current system and would use a tax base supported by a relatively consistent concept of income. In popular discussions, however, the term "fundamental tax reform" has frequently referred to a different type of tax change: replacing the current federal individual and corporate income taxes with a system that taxes consumption but exempts saving. Most taxonomies list three basic types of national-level consumption taxes: value-added taxes; a national sales tax; and a tax on individuals' consumed income. In addition, a prominent "flat tax" proposal would consist of a form of value-added tax imposed at the corporate level and a wage tax at the individual level.

The different forms of consumption taxes differ chiefly in their methods of collection and, as a result, their ease of administration and compliance costs. Their general effect on business taxes, however, would be the same: income from new business investment would be exempt from tax under each form. In the near term, however, income from investment in place at the time of transition would generally be taxed.

National Sales Tax

Turning to specifics, a national retail sales tax would operate much as do the sales taxes imposed by most states: the tax would be imposed on final sales from businesses to consumers; businesses would collect the tax and remit it to the government. In general, business-to-business sales (sales of intermediate goods) would be exempt from the tax; the levy would be applied to imports, but exported goods would be exempt.

To the extent that business inputs are included in the base of a national sales tax, the product to which they contribute would be subject to multiple layers of tax; such cascading would carry the potential of inefficient distortions, diverting resources away from the heavily taxed products. Accordingly, an important task under a national sales tax would be distinguishing between business and non-business uses of purchased items, so as to exempt the former and tax the latter. One possible method of doing so would be to issue exemption certificates to businesses so as to remove their purchases from the tax base. Nonetheless, making the distinction would likely present significant administrative and compliance problems, particularly in the case of items that lend themselves to both business and personal use (e.g., many services). Compliance might also present a problem, given the high tax rate that would likely be necessary to avoid a revenue loss if income taxes were abolished.[19]

Value-Added Tax and "Flat" Tax

As the term implies, value-added taxes (VAT) are levied on the value added by each firm in a good's production process. VATs thus differ in their point of collection from retail sales taxes, but by the final stage of production the cumulative rate of the VAT on an item is the same as that of a sales tax (assuming each is applied uniformly).

There are two general methods by which VATs are administered: credit-invoice and subtraction. Under a credit-invoice method, a business is assessed VAT on its gross receipts, regardless of whether its sales are made to another business or to a final consumer. At the same time, the firms from which it has purchased its inputs provide it with invoices showing the VAT the suppliers have already paid with respect to the inputs. The purchasing firm claims the VAT shown on the invoice as a credit against the VAT on its own sales. As a result, for each firm, the VAT applies only to value added. Under a subtraction-method VAT, tax is levied on a firm's gross receipts after subtracting purchases from other firms. What is left, then, as the base of the tax is the return to capital (profits) and the return to labor (wages)—the value added by the taxed firm. Despite the difference in administration, a subtraction-method VAT and a credit-invoice VAT produce the same tax, assuming they are levied at the same rate. It should also be noted that, as with a sales tax, each is levied on imports, but exports are not included in taxable gross receipts. In the case of the credit-invoice method, an exporting firm receives a tax rebate for taxes paid with respect to its inputs.

A variation on the subtraction-method VAT is the so-called "flat tax"—sometimes termed the Hall-Rabushka proposal after its designers. Under the flat tax, a subtraction-method VAT would be imposed on business—that is, firms would pay a tax on gross receipts minus items purchased from other firms. In contrast to a pure VAT, however, firms would also be permitted to subtract wages from gross income, thus removing from the business-level tax base that portion of the firm's value-added contributed by labor. Individuals, however, would be assessed a tax on wages received, thus bringing the value added by labor back into the tax base, albeit at the individual level.

By the final stage of production, the cumulative rate of a VAT on an item is the same as that of a sales tax, assuming neither contains special allowances and benefits. Thus, their broad economic effects are the same. But since the two types of tax differ in how they are collected, there are differences in compliance and ease of administration. A VAT would impose a higher compliance burden on businesses in general than a retail sales tax; under a VAT, every business would be required to file a tax return, not just businesses in the retail sector. At the same time, a VAT avoids the administrative problem of distinguishing business use of items from personal use. Further, some analysts have argued that small businesses would likely encounter high compliance costs under a national sales tax, and small businesses are relatively numerous in the retail sector. Thus, compliance rates may be higher under a VAT.

Consumed Income Tax

A third type of consumption tax is a tax on consumed income imposed at the individual rather than business level. Individual income consists of consumption plus saving. Thus, individuals would calculate their tax by subtracting saving from their income and paying tax on the residual. Business investments made by individuals would be characterized as saving, and thus an exempt use of income. Thus, for example, an individual's purchases of stock would be deducted from taxable income, as would, say, the purchase of a new machine by a small business owner. Note that an individual consumption tax is defined in terms of the uses of income rather than its source. Thus, it is business investment that is deductible rather than income generated by businesses. However, arithmetic dictates that deducting the cost of a capital investment at the time it is made ("expensing" the investment) produces a tax saving that is identical in present-value terms to exempting the net income the investment produces as it is generated over the investment's lifetime. Thus, deducting business investment on the uses side of the income ledger is the same as exempting income from new investment on the sources side. New business investment bears no burden under an individual consumption tax.

Effects of a Consumption Tax on Business

A consumption tax exempts from its coverage income that is saved, which is the equivalent of exempting investment income. In short, under any form of pure consumption tax—be it a sales tax, a VAT, or an individual consumption tax—business profits are ultimately exempt from tax. As a result, if it is assumed that a consumption tax would not contain its own preferences for special goods or services (an assumption that is perhaps heroic), the various non-neutralities existing under the current system of business taxation would be eliminated. As described in the preceding section on economic efficiency, these include current law's preference of non-corporate investment over the corporate sector, of corporate debt over equity, and of machines and equipment over inventory and structures. If these non-neutralities were eliminated under a consumption tax, business investment—especially corporate investment—could be expected to increase under a consumption tax, as well as equity finance and investment in assets other than equipment. Economic efficiency could potentially increase.

It is worth underlining, however, that it is not the taxation of capital per se that produces these non-neutralities, but the particular shape of capital income taxation that has gradually come into being in the current system. Under a consumption tax, non-neutralities affecting business might be implemented in a different way, but the result might still be distortions in the allocation in business investment. For example, a sales tax or VAT might exempt a particular type of good from taxation, which would favor investment in the sector producing that type of good.

The transition to a consumption tax would likely include significant effects in the short and medium term. Perhaps most importantly, a consumption tax would exempt the return to new investment, but would still apply to income produced by investment in place at the time of the tax's implementation. Note that under none of the types of consumption taxes outlined above would a firm be able to continue to recover the cost of capital in place at the time of transition, either through depreciation or other deductions. At the same time, revenue produced by old investments would be included in the tax base, producing a windfall loss for owners of existing capital. Firms affected most heavily by the taxation of old capital would be older, slow-growing firms. Also, if a uniform consumption tax were adopted and existing business distortions were consequently eliminated, as described above, transition effects would include a shift of resources away from previously favored investment. For example, business sectors where corporate production is intensive would benefit, as would firms with low debt-to-equity ratios and production processes favoring machines and equipment over structures.[20]

A frequently made popular argument for a consumption tax relates to its purported beneficial effects on competitiveness. As described above under the heading "Taxes and Trade," economic theory indicates taxes have little impact on competitiveness as it is popularly understood. However, a specific argument relating to "border tax adjustments" is frequently made in support of consumption taxes, so the argument is worth describing here. The argument—frequently made by businesses—focuses on the fact that foreign firms in VAT countries receive a rebate of the VAT on exports to the United States and elsewhere. Thus, it is argued, foreign firms from VAT countries have a cost advantage over competing U.S. firms. As described in the section on competitiveness, however, taxes or tax-related mechanisms such as VAT rebates do not directly alter the balance of trade. In the particular case of VAT rebates, exchange rate adjustments in response to the rebates act to eliminate any impact on the balance of trade or "competitiveness."

CONCLUSION

While the charts presented earlier in this report show that the level of the corporate tax has generally fallen in the decades since World War II, the basic structure has remained the same: a "classical" system under which the corporate income tax is superimposed on the individual income tax. In 1986, the far-reaching Tax Reform Act implemented reforms within the context of the existing system, broadening its base and reducing rates. In recent years, however, concern about the impact of the system on capital formation and U.S. performance in international markets has stimulated interest in a more substantial structural change, either by adopting tax integration or moving towards a consumption tax.

End Notes

[1] Bonus depreciation was initially provided by the Job Creation and Worker Assistance Act of 2002 (JCWA; P.L. 107- 147). It was increased by the Jobs and Growth Tax Relief and Reconciliation Act of 2003 (JGTRRA; P.L. 108-27) but generally does not apply to property placed in service after 2004. The domestic production deduction was provided by the American Job Creation Act of 2004 (AJCA; P.L. 108-357).

[2] For a more detailed description of the taxation of passthrough entities, see CRS Report RL31538, *Passthrough Organizations Not Taxed As Corporations*, by Jack H. Taylor (out of print, available from the author). See also CRS Report RL32254, *Small Business Tax Benefits: Overview and Economic Rationale*, by Gary Guenther.

[3] U.S. Congressional Budget Office, *Taxing Capital Income: Effective Rates and Approaches to Reform* (Washington: GPO, 2005), p. 19.

[4] An exception is income earned by corporations subject to the alternative minimum tax (AMT). AMT rules in some cases apply differently to corporations compared to individuals.

[5] More precisely, METRs begin by assuming that investments must earn a particular return, after taxes, in order to attract funds from savers. The METR calculation then works backwards, and derives a pre-tax return investments must earn in order to generate the after-tax return required by savers. The difference between the pre-tax and after-tax returns is sometimes referred to as the "tax wedge." An investment's METR consists of the tax wedge divided by the pre-tax return.

[6] For a discussion of factors underlying the variation in METRs, see CRS Report RS21706, *Historical Effective Marginal Tax Rates on Capital Income*, by Jane G. Gravelle.

[7] Tax distortions among assets also persist within the corporate sector. While differential treatment of assets declined under the Tax Reform Act of 1986, subsequent changes in law have reintroduced significant differences in the treatment of equipment, structures, and inventories, with equipment being favored. See CRS Report RL32099, *Capital Income Tax Revisions and Effective Tax Rates*, by Jane G. Gravelle. See also U.S. Congressional Budget Office, *Taxing Capital Income: Effective Rates and Approaches to Reform* (Washington: GPO, 2005), p. 8.

[8] Some economists have concluded that the distortions from taxing capital are so great that the optimal tax on capital from the point of view of economic efficiency and welfare is zero.

Acceptance of this analysis, even in principle, requires a particular theoretical construct that includes, for example, an assumption that individuals have infinitely lived time horizons. But even if this analysis is accepted, it does not necessarily recommend a repeal of capital income taxation for a number of reasons: the unresponsiveness of saving may reduce any distortions; any tax that replaces a tax on capital likely has its own distortions; and the transition costs of moving to an alternative tax may be costly enough to offset any benefit.

[9] For a thorough survey of the empirical studies that have been conducted, see B. Douglas Bernheim, "Taxation and Saving," *Handbook of Public Economics*, vol. 3, Alan J. Auerbach and Martin Feldstein, eds., (Amsterdam: Elsevier, 2002), pp. 1173-1249. Note also that while investment incentives may not result in additional domestic saving, they may attract foreign capital into the domestic economy. The return to foreign capital, however, does not accrue to domestic residents.

[10] For a textbook presentation of this argument, see Andrew B. Abel and Ben S. Bernanke, *Macroeconomics*, 3rd ed. (Reading, MA: Addison-Wesley, 1998), p. 210.

[11] Jane G. Gravelle, "The Corporate Tax: Where Has it Been and Where is it Going?" *National Tax Journal*, vol. 57, Dec. 2004, p. 914.

[12] Arnold H. Harberger, "The Incidence of the Corporation Income Tax," *Journal of Political Economy,* vol. 70, June 1962, pp. 215-240.

[13] See the review of challenges to the Harberger model in Jane G. Gravelle, "The Corporate Income Tax: Economic Issues and Policy Options," *National Tax Journal*, vol. 48, June, 1995, pp. 267-277.

[14] Note, however, that a country's general fiscal position can alter the trade balance. For example, if a country increases its government's budget deficit, real interest rates may rise, leading to an inflow of foreign capital and an expansion of its trade deficit. Thus, to the extent business taxes contribute to total government revenue and the government's overall fiscal stance, they can be said to have an impact on the trade deficit. In this sense, however, they are indistinguishable from other taxes.

[15] For example, even the initial, more theoretically pure, Treasury Department proposals that preceded the 1986 Tax Reform Act stopped short of straightforward taxation of the return to debt.

[16] For estimates of disparities in tax burdens across assets under current law, see CRS Report RL32099, *Capital Income Tax Revisions and Effective Tax Rates*, by Jane G. Gravelle.

[17] CRS has prepared for the Senate Budget Committee a compendium containing explanations and analyses of the various tax expenditures on a biannual basis. The most recent version is U.S. Congress, Senate Committee on the Budget, *Tax Expenditures: Compendium of Background Material on Individual Provisions*, 110th Cong., 2nd sess., December 2008, S. Prt. 110-667 (Washington: GPO, 2008).

[18] For a more comprehensive discussion and analysis of integration, see CRS Report RL31597, *The Taxation of ividend Income: An Overview and Economic Analysis of the Issues*, by Jane G. Gravelle.

[19] For more detailed discussions of how a national sales tax might operate in practice, see John L. Mikesell, "The American Retail Sales Tax: Considerations on Their Structure, Operations, and Potential as a Foundation for a Federal Sales Tax," *National Tax Journal*, vol. 50, Mar. 1997, pp. 149-165, and Martin Sullivan, *Flat Taxes and Consumption Taxes: A Guide to the Debate* (Washington: American Institute of Certified Public Accountants, 1995), pp. 11-18.

[20] For a more detailed analysis of the impact of fundamental tax reform on business, see CRS Report RL32603, *The Flat Tax, Value-Added Tax, and National Retail Sales Tax: Overview of the Issues*, by Jane G. Gravelle.

In: Federal Taxation
Editor: Jaclyn N. Prichard

ISBN: 978-1-61324-102-8

Chapter 4

SMALL BUSINESS AND THE EXPIRATION OF THE 2001 TAX RATE REDUCTIONS: ECONOMIC ISSUES*

Jane G. Gravelle

SUMMARY

At the end of 2010, the lower income tax rates provided in 2001 were to expire. The President had proposed to extend most tax cuts, but to continue higher rates for couples with income over $250,000 and singles with income over $200,000. The most important element of this proposal, as measured by revenue effect, is allowing the top rates of 33% and 35% to expire, when they would have risen to 36% and 36.9%. P.L. 111-312, enacted in December 2010, extended all tax cuts for two years, through 2012, delaying the consideration of which tax cuts to retain.

Some critics of allowing the tax rates to rise express concerns about possible negative effects on small business owners' hiring and the dampening effect on job creation. This view is buttressed by a popular conception that small businesses are responsible for the majority, perhaps the vast majority, of new jobs.

The first issue addressed is how well retaining the lower levels of the top two rates target small business. Two aspects of targeting are considered: the fraction of small businesses affected by the rate changes and the fraction of

* This is an edited, reformatted and augmented version of Congressional Research Services publication R41392, dated January 6, 2011.

revenue gain accruing to taxpayers other than these small businesses. The results suggest that only a small fraction of businesses would be affected, around 2% to 3%. They also suggest that 80% of the reduced taxes are likely to accrue to non-businesses income and almost 90% to either non-business income or businesses without employees.

The claim that small businesses are the primary creators of jobs is based on research published originally in the 1980s. More recent research has revealed some methodological deficiencies in these original studies and suggests that small businesses contribute only slightly more jobs than other firms relative to their employment share. Moreover, this differential is not due to hiring by existing small firms, but rather to startups, which tend to be small. Some critics also question whether small business jobs should be encouraged because they tend to be lower paid, with fewer benefits and more turnover. Yet, small businesses may offer employment to workers with less education or other characteristics that lead to difficulty finding employment with larger firms.

In addition to targeting efficiency and job creation issues, there is uncertainty about the effects of taxation on small businesses. An extensive literature suggests that higher taxes have no effect or actually encourage self-employment. Researchers speculate that higher taxes may lead individuals to select self-employment because the opportunities for tax evasion and avoidance are greater. In addition, taxes reduce risk (the variance in return) and greater variance in earnings likely occurs in self-employment. Evidence of effects of taxes on existing firms' hiring is limited.

Perhaps the most important issue concerns job creation as a policy justification. In the long run, there is no need to address job creation as the market economy naturally generates jobs (although targeted programs, such as those for disadvantaged workers, may improve efficiency). In times of recession, the government may need fiscal stimulus, but the purpose of this stimulus is generally to increase aggregate demand. The most effective approaches are direct spending and tax cuts and transfers to lower income individuals who are more likely to spend. Tax cuts for high income individuals or business are less likely to be spent and are less effective as a stimulus.

There may be justifications for favoring small business, although small businesses, especially businesses owned by high income individuals, are already subject to favorable treatment. Tax policy might be most appropriately formulated in the light of any imperfections in the economy which justify preferential treatment.

INTRODUCTION

At the end of 2010, the lower income tax rates provided in the 2001 tax cuts were to expire. President Obama had proposed to extend most of the income tax cuts, but to continue some higher tax rates for couples with income over $250,000 and singles with income over $200,000. The most important element of this proposal, as measured by revenue effect, is allowing the top two rates of 33% and 35% to expire. These rates would have risen to 36% and 36.9%. This proposal would have raised $369 billion over FY2011-FY2020, about half of the total from all proposals for not extending tax cuts for these high income taxpayers.[1] At the end of December, P.L. 111-312 extended all tax cuts for two years. Thus the issue of extending the tax cuts will continue as an issue in the 112th Congress.

Although a variety of issues surround this option, this report focuses on a particular issue, the effect on small business owners, and in turn, the potential effects on employment. Some critics of allowing the tax rates to rise express concerns about possible negative effects on small business owners' hiring and the dampening effect on job creation. This argument is buttressed by a popular conception that small businesses are responsible for the majority, perhaps the vast majority, of new jobs. In some cases, this issue appears to relate to the short-term, which has been addressed, for now, with the temporary extension. If the economy continues with high unemployment, as some project, the short-term issue may re-emerge. In some cases the issue appears to relate to longer-term issues and will be relevant to the question of permanent policy.

The first section of this report addresses the effects of the changes in top rates, and how well these revisions target small businesses. Two aspects of targeting are considered: the fraction of small businesses affected by the rate changes and the fraction of revenue gain accruing to taxpayers other than these small businesses. The results suggest that only a small fraction of small businesses will be affected, around 2% to 3%. They also suggest that 80% of the reduced taxes are likely to accrue to non-businesses income and about 90% to non-business income or businesses without employees.

The second section of the report reviews the claim that small businesses are the primary creators of jobs. This perception is based on research published originally in the 1980s. More recent research has revealed some methodological deficiencies in these original studies and suggests that small businesses contribute only slightly more jobs than other firms relative to their employment share. In addition, this differential is not due to hiring by existing small firms, but rather to startups, which tend to be small. This section also briefly summarizes issues raised by some researchers about the quality of jobs in the small business sector.

The third section reviews the evidence on the effect of taxes on entrepreneurship and self-employment. The results of these studies are mixed, but overall they do not suggest that lower taxes are likely to increase self-employment.

The following section discusses perhaps the most important issue to consider, job creation as a policy justification for targeted provisions. The basic economics of market equilibrium indicate that, in the long run, there is no need for the government to intervene in the creation of jobs. In the short run, intervention is appropriate during a recession, but tax cuts to businesses and high income individuals are not likely to be very effective for this purpose.

The final section briefly summarizes the current benefits and penalties for small businesses in the tax code and general justifications for preferential tax treatment.[2]

THE EFFECTS ON SMALL BUSINESSES OF ALLOWING THE TWO TOP RATES TO EXPIRE: TARGET EFFICIENCY

Given an objective of benefiting small businesses, how well would retaining the top two current tax rates be targeted to small businesses? There are two parts to this question: the fraction of small businesses in the country affected by the tax change (which indicates whether most of the target is being reached) and the share of the tax benefit falling on activities other than those targeted (which indicates how much is being spent on income outside of business).

Before addressing these data questions, it is important to recognize what types of business income appear on individual tax returns, especially as subsequent analysis will also focus on the activities of different forms of business organizations.

Unincorporated businesses, or businesses taxed as if they were not incorporated, with owners' income subject to the individual income tax, generally operate as sole proprietors, partnerships, or Subchapter S firms. These businesses are also referred to as pass-through or flow-through entities. Sole proprietorships have one owner, while partnerships are businesses with two or more owners. Some types of partnerships have attributes of corporations, mainly limited liability (limited partnerships and limited liability corporations). Finally individuals or partners can operate as Subchapter S corporations, which are incorporated but treated, for tax purposes, as unincorporated businesses.

According to data from the Internal Revenue Service, there were 32.1 million businesses in 2007, most of them sole proprietorships. Firms include 1.9 million corporations, 4 million Subchapter S corporations, 3 million partnerships (0.7 million general partnerships, 0.5 million limited liability partnerships, and 1.8 million limited liability corporations), and 23.1 million sole proprictors.[3]

While businesses with flow-through income treatment are not all necessarily small, and most corporations are small, these flow-through businesses (proprietorships, partnerships or Subchapter S corporations), for purposes of analyzing tax effects, are treated as a proxy for small businesses in the data presented in this report.

In reviewing data on the targeting of these rate cuts, several factors qualify the results of some calculations and are useful to enumerate at this point. The first is that not all high income taxpayers who appear, based on income, to be affected by the rates changes will be, because of the alternative minimum tax (AMT). Some data sources account for this effect and some do not. Since these tax rates are not changing, the significant share of high income taxpayers who would otherwise pay tax at the 36% or 39.6% rates will pay the AMT and their taxes will not be affected.

The second is that a significant share of taxpayers and income at high income levels are recipients of passive rather than active income. An example of passive income might be rental income as a limited partner in a real estate leasing operation. Recipients of passive income through partnerships and Subchapter S corporations are similar to shareholders of corporations: they do not actively run the business or make hiring decisions.

The third is that some businesses experience losses, and there is no income to be subject to tax. Whether calculations include businesses with losses will have consequences for the estimates.

Finally, the vast majority of small businesses, almost 80%, do not have employees. Although some limited evidence will be discussed, it is unlikely that a small tax reduction for these non-employer firms would induce these firms to hire.

What Share of Small Businesses Are Affected?

Small business owners would be expected to be relatively more affected by tax rate changes that apply to the top brackets than other taxpayers because they are more concentrated in the higher income brackets than the remainder of the population. Table 1 compares the share of all returns in high income classes (which are roughly equivalent to the taxpayers potentially subject to the top tax rates) to the share of business returns. Business income is reported in two basic categories: income from business or profession, which reflects sole proprietorships, and income from partnerships and Subchapter S firms.

As Table 1 indicates, returns for businesses are more concentrated in higher income classes than returns in general, and this effect is particularly the case for partnership and Subchapter S firms. The $200,000 and above adjusted gross income class includes some taxpayers who would not be affected by the President's proposals (because their incomes would not place them in these top rates), which indicates a share of less than 9.6% of small businesses would be affected. As will be shown below, the shares of returns affected subject to the top two rates are also significantly reduced because of the AMT. The shares can also be affected by how returns with losses are treated.

Table 1. Share of Tax Returns in High Income Classes, 2008

Income Class	Share of All Returns	Share of Returns With Business Income or Loss	Share of Sole Proprietorship	Share of Partnership and Subchapter S
>$200,000	3.1%	9.6%	5.1%	22.4%
>$500,000	0.6%	2.7%	1.0%	7.4%

Source: Statistics of Income, Internal Revenue Service, Individual Income Tax, http://www.irs.gov/taxstats/ indtaxstats/article/0,,id=98123,00.html.

The Joint Committee on Taxation, the Department of Treasury, and the Urban-Brookings Tax Policy Center have provided information on the share of returns and income of small business either in the higher income categories or subject to the top two tax rates.

The Joint Committee on Taxation (JCT) estimates that in 2011, 3% of taxpayers with net positive small business income (about 750,000 taxpayers) would be subject to the two top marginal tax rates under the President's proposal.[4] This estimate does not include taxpayers with net losses. JCT also estimates that about 50% of business income will be reported on returns with these marginal tax rates (with aggregate income approximately $1 trillion). This study included income from rents and royalties, and estates and trusts, as well as Subchapter S, partnership, and sole proprietorship business income in estimating shares.

A Treasury Study in 2007, prepared for an economic competitiveness conference, had a chapter on pass-though entities, which included data on the share of business income by high income taxpayers. This study focused on examining high income taxpayers with business income and did not adjust for the alternative minimum tax, so the numbers are comparable to those in Table 1. As with the JCT study, it focused on returns with positive net income. It included ordinary income from partnerships, sole proprietorships, and Subchapter S corporations, as well as capital gains from partnerships, Subchapter S corporations and estates and trusts. It provided, however, some important information of the effects of including passive versus active income. Some partners or shareholders of Subchapter S corporations are not active business owners. It also provided the share of returns and income in which income was reasonably large relative to wages (thus excluding those taxpayers whose income was a minor part of earnings). As shown in Table 2, the shares of returns falling in the income ranges of the top brackets are consistent with Table 1, but neither include the effect of the AMT and, therefore, both overstate the share subject to the two top tax rates.

Table 2. Shares of Returns and Income In High Income Brackets, 2006

	Share of Total Pass Through Entities	Share of Pass-Throughs with Active Income	Share of Business Income Greater than 50% of Wages
Returns	27.5 million	18.3 million	11.9 million
Top Two Rates	8%	7%	9%
Top Rate	4%	4%	5%
Share of Income	$938 billion	$762 billion	$880 billion
Top Two Rates	72%	57%	69%
Top Rate	61%	46%	60%

Source: U.S. Department of Treasury, Treasury Conference on Business Taxation and Global Competitiveness, Background Paper, July 23, 2007, http://www.treas.gov/press/releases/reports/07230%20r.pdf.

Table 2 also indicates that a significant portion of returns (over a third) and income (19%) are passive.[5] Excluding passive income slightly lowers the share of returns in the top brackets (from 8% to 7%) and significantly lowers the share of income (from 72% to 57%).

Table 2 also shows that a significant share of income will accrue to individuals where it is a minor part of their income, which might occur with a small consulting business for someone whose main source of income is wages.

The Urban-Brookings Tax Policy Center has also calculated the share of business returns and the share of business income falling into the top brackets. Their results are similar to those reported by the Joint Committee on Taxation. They also consider only taxpayers with positive income, and take into account the alternative minimum tax. As shown in Table 3, their results also indicate shares in the different rates, showing that most of the returns and income are in the top bracket. (For example, 3.6% of returns are subject to one of the top two rates, but 2.5% of returns are subject to the top rate, so that 1.2 % of returns pay tax at the second highest rate.)

Table 3. Share of Business Returns and Income in the Top Two Rate Brackets, 2011

	Total	Proprietorship	Partnership	Subchapter S
Returns	20.3 million	16.4 million	2.9 million	2.8 million
Top Two Rates	3.6%	1.4%	12.9%	13.5%
Top Rate	2.5%	0.9%	9.8%	10.0%
Income	$905 billion	$337 billion	$251 billion	$342 billion
Top Two Rates	44.8%	11.3%	58.5%	66.6%
Top Rate	40.7%	9.3%	52.9%	61.7%

Source: Urban-Brookings Tax Policy Center, Table T10-0211, http://www.taxpolicycenter.org/numbers/displayatab.cfm?Docid=2787&DocTypeID=7.

The Tax Policy Center also reports separately for sole proprietorships, partnerships and Subchapter S firms. As also was suggested by data in Table 1, high income business taxpayers are responsible for larger shares of partners and shareholders of Subchapter S income. Table 3 reports a slightly smaller share in the top rate brackets for partnerships than for Subchapter S firms, but the shares are significantly less for sole proprietorships.

The data in Table 3 indicate that among the taxpayers subject to the top rates, 23% are sole proprietors, 38% are partners, and 39% are shareholders of Subchapter S corporations. By contrast, about 80% of all returns with business income are sole proprietorship returns, with the remainder divided relatively evenly between partnership and Subchapter S.[6]

As is clear from these tables, adjusting for the AMT is important in calculating the fraction of businesses which would be subject to the top tax rates, as JCT estimates and Table 3 indicate a share of around 3% while the estimates in Table 1 and Table 2 indicate a share of 9%.

In addition, the calculations in Table 2 and Table 3 and by the JCT estimate the distribution of taxpayers with positive income, while the calculations in Table 1 include both returns with net positive income and returns with losses. One can also make the argument that the universe of businesses include those with losses, but only those with gains would be subject to the higher tax rates.[7]

Table 4 returns to the aggregate data in Table 1 and makes some of these adjustments to examine the share. First, it confines the numerator only to taxable returns (while retaining all businesses returns in the denominator). This correction makes very little difference to the outcome, however. Second, it also adjusts, separately and in combination, for including only returns with positive income in the numerator and for the AMT.[8] When the AMT adjustment is made alone, the results are similar to those for the Tax Policy Center data in Table 3. Including only returns with positive income in the numerator lowers the share measurably, and in combination with the AMT, reduces the share from 3.5% to 2.5%.

Another correction, when considering the universe of small businesses, is to add corporate returns to the denominator. That is, corporate returns are not affected by these individual tax rate changes, but they do constitute part of the universe of small businesses. Of the 1.9 million corporate returns, the vast majority would be considered small business. How many should be added to the denominator depends on the definition of small business. According to Census data, there are approximately 1.3 million corporations (with the remaining 0.6 million probably non-employer businesses, that is, businesses with no employees).[9] Many sources, including the Census Bureau, use firms with less than 500 employees as a standard for a small business. Since there are only 18,000 firms that have 500 or more employees, all of the 1.9 million would be added to the denominator of the ratio. This correction would reduce the 2.6% figure to 2.5%, and the 1.1% figure to 1%. If, for example, firms with 9 or fewer employees were considered small, the effects would be similar: the total of small corporations would be 1.6 million.

In addition to these small businesses reported on tax returns, small businesses that do not file tax returns, either because they had sufficient losses or because of evasion, would increase the size of the denominator and lower the share.

The implication of this analysis is that only a small fraction of small businesses are affected by the two top rates, ranging from 2.5% to 3.5%.[10]

Table 4. Share of Businesses In High Income Classes, Alternative Assumptions, 2008

Income	Share of Returns with Business Income	Share of Sole Proprietorship	Share of Partnership and Subchapter S
Taxable Returns Only			
>$200,000	9.5%	5.1%	22.2%
>$500,000	2.7%	1.0%	7.4%
Taxable and Positive Returns Only			
>$200,000	7.2%	3.8%	16.8%
>$500,000	2.1%	0.8%	5.7%
Taxable Returns Plus AMT Correction			
>$200,000	3.5%	1.7%	8.4%
>$500,000	1.5%	0.6%	4.1%
Taxable and Positive Returns Plus AMT Correction			
>$200,000	2.6%	1.3%	6.4%
>$500,000	1.1%	0.4%	3.1%

Source: Statistics of Income, Internal Revenue Service, Individual Income Tax.

What Share of the Tax Benefit Does Not Go to Small Business Operations?

The second aspect of the targeting is what share of the tax cut is likely to go to business income. The Tax Policy Center has estimated that 26% of income appears on returns whose highest bracket would be 36% and 33.4% of income on returns in the 39.6% bracket is business income. Weighting the two indicates a share of 33%.[11]

Although this share suggests that two thirds of the tax benefit does not affect the targeted population, there are two reasons to expect that the estimate of the share benefitting businesses may be too high. First, a significant share of this business income does not come from operating an active business but from a passive investment. Based on the share of income that is passive reported in Table 2, this estimate would be reduced from 36% to 21%.

The second reason is that a significant share of businesses are non-employer businesses: according to Census data, out of 27 million businesses, 21 million are businesses that have no employees.[12] Thus, it is unlikely that a slight reduction in income tax rates for non-employer businesses are likely to induce these firms to hire.[13] If the 21% share were multiplied by the ratio of all employer businesses (6 million) to all businesses (27 million), the fraction of the benefit going to small businesses with workers would be less than 5%. Unfortunately, there is no information available about the characteristics of these high income returns relative to the basic population, but there is some reason to reduce the expected share of income affected to reflect income of non-employer firms who are unlikely to hire employees. In the Appendix, this issue is explored with available data; the results suggest a reduction to around 12%.

JOB CREATION AND JOB QUALITY IN SMALL BUSINESSES

The popular idea that small business is responsible for most new jobs in the economy dates from a study by Birch in 1981.[14] This study found that firms with less than 100 employees, which represented about 35% of the labor force, created 8 out of 10 jobs over the 1969-1976 period.

Similar figures are still cited occasionally. For example, Headd reports, using the same methodology, that small businesses, defined as firms with less than 500 employees, who employ half of workers, accounted for 90% of net job creation from 1993 to 2006.[15]

The Birch findings have led to a series of studies questioning the methodology that led to these results. In general, the issues that might be raised about the Birch findings include the use of establishment rather than firm data and a statistical problem referred to as "regression to the mean." Establishments may be individual firms, or they may be outlets of large firms (e.g., the local Walmart store, which is part of a large corporation).

The first study, by Armington and Odle, addressed the establishment versus firm issue.[16] They found that the firms studied by Birch accounted for about 38% of net new jobs, roughly in proportion to their numbers, for 1978-1980. They suggested that Birch had counted as small firms businesses that were outlets of larger firms.

Brown, Hamilton, and Medoff also report, based on a study by the Small Business Administration, that the Birch numbers overstated the share of jobs created, finding that these firms accounted for 56% of new jobs.[17] They found considerable variation across different time periods. In some intervals these small firms accounted for virtually all growth. On average, firms with less than 100 employees seemed to account for about half of jobs created from 1976 to 1986, more than their share in the labor force in 1980 of 35%. (These shares are similar to those of the period 1969-76.) Firms with less than 500 employees accounted for about 60% of net new jobs over the same time period, with a labor force share of about 50%.

These authors also had some other interesting insights into the figures on job creation by small firms. Although the data suggest that small businesses in general created new jobs in excess of their share of the labor force, there were two important qualifications to this observation. First, part of the growth reflected the fact that industries that tended to be dominated by small firms had been growing. The increased jobs by new firms may not have been so much because small firms were doing better than larger ones, but rather because the industries in which small firms operated were growing, perhaps for unrelated reasons.

Second, they point out that most of the jobs were created by new firms, which tend, of course, to be small (firms are not usually "born" large). According to Brown, et al., the majority of these jobs will not persist because many of the firms will fail; from 60% to 80% within the first few years. The data reflect a blending of small firms and new firms.

Economists were also concerning themselves with a problem referred to as "regression to the mean." This problem arises in many contexts and refers to observations that are away from their means but moving toward them. In the context of small and large firms, the problem is that Birch and other researchers classified firms by their size in each year to assign changes in employment size. However, if firms are subject to shocks (either negative or positive) more firms that have suffered a negative shock will be in the small group and more firms that have had a positive shock will be in the large group. Thus, even if all the firms are the same permanent size, the firms identified as "small" firms will be growing and the firms identified as "large" will be declining.

This phenomenon led to a communication to the *Journal of Economic Literature* by the eminent economist Milton Friedman, published in 1992, criticizing researchers for not recognizing this problem and mentioning the small business job creation research as an illustration.[18] At the time this communication was published, researchers were working to find a data set and test this effect. This research ultimately led to a book by Davis, Haltiwanger, and Schuh.[19] They used longitudinal data on manufacturing that followed firms over a period of time. Instead of just examining firms and classifying them by size, they used average size or terminal size. All firm sizes were declining, but they found the smallest declines in the largest firms. These results contrasted with the results using Birch's method on their data, which showed positive growth rates in the smaller firms and negative growth for larger firms. Their research appeared to show not only that regression-to-the-mean was important quantitatively, but also showed that it reversed the findings.

Following the Davis et al. study, Neumark, Wall, and Zhang examined this issue with a different data set that included all industries (although it was confined to firms operating in California) over the 1992-2004 period.[20] They found correcting for regression-to-the mean to be quantitatively quite important but it did not reverse the direction of changes. For example, without the correction, using base size, employment in the smallest firms, with 0 to 10 employees, grew by 22% and employment in firms with 50,000 or more declined by 3%. With average firm size classification, employment in the small firms grew by 3.2% and employment in the largest declined by 1.6%. They also cite other research and suggest that the change in direction for the Davis, Haltiwanger, and Schuh study may have been due to the specific industry, manufacturing.

Haltiwanger, Jarmin, and Miranda use a national data base to further explore this issue.[21] As with earlier studies, they found regression-to-the-mean to be a significant problem. After correcting for that, they find differences across firm sizes, with a general tendency for smaller firms to grow slightly faster, although the differences are generally small and job growth rates do not decline continually as firm size rises. Job growth rates are much larger for the smallest business (0 to 4) class. They then decline with larger firm size, up to 19 employees, rise up to 250 employees, are almost constant up to 2,500 employees, and then decline. Perhaps more importantly, the authors find any relationship disappears with controls for age. That is, it is new firms (which are generally small) that are growing faster, not mature small firms.

Headd's paper also reports, based on data using methods controlling for regression to the mean, that firms with less than 500 employees are responsible for 65% of employment growth, although it is difficult to determine from his exposition whether these results are reflecting establishments or firms.[22] It is, at any rate, a marked contrast from the 90% figure he cites without controlling for these effects.

The absolute share of new jobs ascribed to small businesses depends on how small business is defined. Birch defined small businesses as firms with less than 100; the U.S. Bureau of the Census defines small businesses as firms with less than 500 employees; and the Small Business Administration has different sizes for different industries. Recent health legislation enacted in 2010, seeking to exempt small businesses from mandates, placed the cut-off at 50 employees. Headd's data are divided into three classes: less than 20, between 20 and 499, and 500 and over. The smallest class, less than 20, was responsible for 22% of net new jobs.[23]

In sum, the research on small business and job growth does not support the notion that small businesses produce a significantly larger share of net new jobs than their share of employment, and the importance of those jobs as an overall share of job growth depends on the definition of small business.

Brown, Hamilton, and Medoff also raise questions about the quality of small business jobs.[24] They point out that jobs in small firms tend to pay lower wages, have fewer fringe benefits, have poorer working conditions, and tend to be less secure than jobs in larger firms. The rates of creation and destruction for smaller (or younger firms that tend to be small) are large. Similar points have been made by other researchers as well. For example, Davis, Haltiwanger and Schuh document the greater turnover in small firms in the manufacturing sector.[25] Headd, while acknowledging these aspects of small business jobs, also notes that the small business sector fills a labor supply niche, of individuals who are more likely to be minorities and have lower educational qualifications.[26] These individuals might have more difficulty finding better jobs in any case. Therefore, it is not clear that the quality of jobs in the small business sector is a justification for either higher or lower taxes.

THE EFFECT OF TAXES ON SMALL BUSINESS

How do taxes affect small business? Given the evidence that more job growth arises from new firms, evidence on the choice of self-employment may be more important than evidence on the behavior of existing firms. An extensive empirical literature on this issue is mixed, but largely suggests that higher tax rates are more likely to encourage, rather than discourage, self-employment.

Schuetze and Bruce review 21 studies of the effects of taxes on employment using a variety of data sets and statistical approaches.[27] Of these studies, 11 found that higher tax rates increased self-employment, two found that they decreased self-employment, and seven found no statistically significant relationship. One study focused on the degree of progressivity in the tax system rather than the level of taxes, and found that a progressive tax system discouraged self-employment.

The studies cover a range of approaches. Eight of the studies used aggregate time series data (for the United States, in most cases) with three studies finding positive effects on self employment for higher tax rates, two finding negative effects, and three finding no effect. Four studies examined cross sections of individuals (comparing tax rates and choice of employment of individuals at one point in time), with three finding a positive effect and one no effect. There are difficulties with both of these approaches that can often be addressed with panel studies (which follow individuals over time) or repeated cross sections. The study of progressivity was of this type. Of the remaining five studies in this category, four found that higher tax rates increased self employment, and one found no effect. Finally, three studies examined the effect of differential state tax rates, with two finding no effect and one a positive effect for higher taxes.

Four additional studies have been released subsequent to this review. Garret and Wall examined state panel data and found no statistically significant effect.[28] Bruce and Deskins examined state tax rates and found no effect of state income tax rates on state entrepreneurship rates, although they found that higher rates slightly reduce the state's share of entrepreneurs.[29] Bruce a Mohsin, using time series data, found negative but quantitatively small effects on entrepreneurship rates.[30] They suggest that it would take a prohibitively large tax rate change to generate a noticeable change in self employment. Gurley-Calvez and Bruce, examining the exit of individuals from self employment, find that cuts in the wage tax, holding employment tax rates constant, would increase exits from self employment, while cuts in self employment rates, holding the wage tax rate constant, would decrease exits.[31] Based on magnitudes, an across-the- board tax cut would increase entrepreneurial longevity.

While these four studies did not find the positive effects that dominated previous studies, the effects were often insignificant. Thus, on the whole, the research suggests that higher tax rates are not likely to decrease self-employment, and could increase it.

There are two reasons one might expect higher tax rates to encourage self-employment, and these are reasons often advanced by researchers. First, self-employment offers greater opportunities to avoid or evade taxes, and avoidance and evasion are more valuable the higher the marginal tax rates.[32] The second reason is that earnings tend to vary more among the self-employed, and higher tax rates reduce the variance of earnings. That is, although expected earnings are taxed, the variation in those earnings is reduced because the government's tax causes it to act as a partner in the business, bearing some of the risk and receiving some of the return.[33]

In contrast to the large body of research on self-employment choice, there is little research on the effects of tax changes on the investments or hiring decisions of existing small firms. Carroll, Holtz-Eakin, Rider, and Rosen used panel data to examine the behavior of firms without employees before and after the Tax Reform Act of 1986, where high income taxpayers had very deep cuts in tax rates. [34] Of particular interest are the estimates of the effects on hiring labor. Since the costs of labor are deductible, tax rates would matter only if the employer expanded the scope of his efforts or investment to increase the size of the firm. They compared high tax rate and low tax rate individuals. Based on their findings, retaining the top two tax rates would, as compared to allowing them to expire, increase workers hired by 6/10 of 1% due to the increase in the probability of hiring, and increase either workers or wages of those firms who already have workers by 9/10 of 1% within four years.[35]

With only one study, one cannot easily rely on the results, particularly since there are limitations to this type of study. One reservation about the estimates is that they seem quite large as a behavioral response, especially for the response of initial non-employer firms to hire workers.[36] Since there is no direct effect on the incentive to hire workers from the changes in the owners tax rate, the increased hiring should derive from the increased effort of the owner or from cash flow effects. The study tested for the latter effect and found no relationship, but never examined the effect on the labor supply of owners. Moreover, in other cases where analysis was based on the 1986 tax reform and estimates were made based on tax changes (especially those that moved in the other direction), elasticities were found to be overstated. Reliance on these results might have to wait until a similar analysis is performed on the 1993 tax increase or the 2001 tax decrease.[37]

The empirical evidence suggests that tax rates have small, uncertain, and possibly unexpected effects on the formation of small business, and given only one study, it is premature to conclude that raising taxes of the owner would decrease hiring in existing firms.

IS JOB CREATION A JUSTIFICATION?

Is lowering taxes, or keeping taxes lower for small business, if there were evidence that tax cuts would be effective, justified by job creation objectives? This issue is perhaps the central one, since all of the other effects do not matter for the purpose of job creation if the answer to that question is no.

In answering this question, it is important to distinguish between longer run policies during periods of full employment and short run policies in a recession.

First, consider the long run. Economic theory suggests that there is no reason to view general job creation as a long run objective of government policies. The economy can generate the jobs needed by the natural process of growth and market adjustment. In 1961 and in 1991 the unemployment rate was the same, 6.7%. Employment, however, rose from 66 million to 117 million.[38] Employment tends to grow steadily; the unemployment rate fluctuates. Long term jobs policies, therefore, should not be aimed at increasing jobs (which at full employment will only lead to inflation), although they can be designed to reduce structural or frictional unemployment (such as improving the skills of disadvantaged workers).

Federal policies may, of course, be needed to smooth out short-term business cycles, but even in these cases it is the aggregate stance of fiscal policy that should be evaluated with respect to job creation, and not a specific program. The short term policy issue, therefore, becomes one of choosing to use resources by determining which type of stimulus is most effective. In general, research suggests that when using fiscal policy to stimulate the economy, direct spending and reducing taxes or increasing transfers to lower income individuals is likely to be most effective. The objective of tax cuts to stimulate the underemployed economy is generally to increase demand, since insufficient demand is the fundamental problem. For fiscal policy, money provided either through spending or tax cuts is only effective if it is spent, and high income taxpayers are probably the least likely to spend. Similarly tax cuts provided for businesses are also likely to be relatively ineffective.[39]

Note that this issue of effectiveness of a stimulus does not depend on where jobs were lost or on evidence from past recessions. Headd, for example, discusses the greater job loss in a recession and gain in a recovery of small businesses.[40] But these contractions and expansions derive from reductions in aggregate demand which tend to affect some industries differently from others (e.g., industries that produce durable goods or goods that are less likely to be necessities). To stimulate the economy with spending or tax cuts requires changes that will be spent initially, and which will naturally increase demand in those sectors that have contracted the most. Trying to deal with sectoral differences by targeting tax cuts to those sectors will likely not succeed if they do not increase spending.

OTHER JUSTIFICATIONS FOR SPECIAL TAX PROVISIONS AND TREATMENT OF SMALL BUSINESS

As the findings in this report suggest, across-the-board tax cuts for high income individuals are not efficiently targeted to small businesses. It is possible to design more focused provisions. However, two important issues should be considered in evaluating more carefully designed provisions. The first is whether small businesses are currently favored or disfavored by the tax law. The second is whether there are justifications for favorable treatment.

In general, small businesses, particularly high-income small businesses, are tax favored compared to large corporations.[41] They are able to use pass-through forms of operation and do not have to pay a separate corporate tax. If they operate as a corporation, they benefit from graduated corporate rates, and they have a variety of special tax benefits. One of these benefits, the ability to immediately deduct the cost of investment in equipment, leads to an effective elimination of tax on the return to this type of investment. Also, as noted earlier, small firms are able to engage more freely in tax evasion. Two aspects of the tax rules may impose a burden, however. The first is the imposition of payroll taxes on all business income, not just labor income. This effect, however, is far more significant for lower- and middle-income small businesses because the old age, survivors, and disability insurance tax base is capped. In addition, additional taxes are associated with additional benefits. Moreover, passive investment income is scheduled to be taxed under Medicare, which has no ceiling, under the health reform proposals.[42] The second is that, because of economies of scale, tax compliance costs are a smaller share of income for large firms than for small ones. In general, most researchers conclude that small businesses are favored relative to large ones.

Is there a justification for providing favorable tax treatment for small business other than job creation? In addition to tax compliance costs, justifications advanced for favoring small businesses include the argument that small businesses are important contributors to economic innovation and technological advance, small businesses undertake greater risks, and small businesses have more difficulty raising capital. While a more detailed examination of these issues is beyond the scope of this report, all three have been questioned by economists as arguments to justify general tax benefits, because of lack of merit in the argument, inefficient targeting, or both.[43] If this favorable treatment is not justified, then the tax system already distorts the allocation of resources away from larger firms and towards smaller ones. If it is justified, it would probably be more efficient to target such issues. For example, if innovation is the issue, tax subsidies should be directed to research and development. If there is a market failure in the capital markets, expanding small business loan guarantees might be more appropriate. If encouraging risk is desirable, provisions aimed at that problem, such as longer loss carryback periods, could be considered. If tax compliance by small business is an issue, expanded cash accounting methods may be helpful.

CONCLUSION

This report has examined the justification for retaining the lower rates for the top two tax rates because of concerns that allowing them to rise will reduce job creation by small businesses. An important reservation about such a justification is that lowering the top tax rates benefits only a small share (3% or so) of businesses, and 80% or more of the tax cut's benefits do not accrue to business. As well as lack of target efficiency, evidence on the role of small business in job creation, the effects of tax changes on small business behavior, and the likelihood this provision would not be an effective demand stimulus suggest that the formulation of small business policies should be informed and guided by any market failures that may exist.

APPENDIX. ESTIMATING THE SHARE OF NON-EMPLOYER FIRMS

This appendix explores the issue of whether the share of the tax cut going to businesses should be reduced by the share of non-employer firms. With no reduction, the results presented earlier indicate that 79% of the tax cut accrues to taxpayers other than businesses, whereas with a full reduction, over 95% accrues to other taxpayers.

Two reservations arise about applying these general figures to high income taxpayers. The first is whether there are differences, given the same type of business operation, between high tax and low tax business owners. The Carroll, et al., study of proprietorships with and without workers found a very similar ratio of firms without employees among low income and high income taxpayers (78% and 79%).[44]

The second is that the composition of business by organizational form differs in the case of high tax rate recipients of business income from the general population. Since it seems more likely that multiple owner businesses will have employees, we adjust the businesses recipients, after removing passive income, for the share that appear to be single owner firms.

To address this second issue, first consider the industry distribution and number of partners and shareholders for non-employer firms as a group, sole proprietorships, partnerships, and subchapter S firms. These distributions are listed in Table A-1 (Non-employer firms), Table A-2 (Sole Proprietorships), Table A-3 (Partnerships), and Table A-4 (Subchapter S Firms), which also provide references to data sources for each type of firm. Proprietorships have a very similar industry distribution to non-employer firms, not surprising as they dominate firms. Partnerships are significantly different (with a much larger share in finance and real estate) and Subchapter S firms have a distribution closer to the non-employer firms than to partnerships, with somewhat more of their business in trade and construction (as well as finance and real estate) and somewhat less in services.

According to data on passive income in Table 2, 36% of high income recipients of pass through income receive passive income. Most of those recipients are likely to be in partnerships, as supported by the much larger share of partners in finance, insurance and real estate in that category (61%) as compared to proprietorships (9%) and Subchapter S firms (17%). In addition, the partnership data provide information on the number of partners in general partnerships, limited partnerships, and limited liability companies. Presuming that these latter two types of firms provide largely passive income, they account for 85% of partners. Also, according to Table 2 high income pass-through owners are allocated 23% to proprietorships, 38% to partners, and 39% to Subchapter S shareholders. By assigning 32% of passive recipients to partnerships (0.85 times 38%) to partnerships and the remaining 4% to Subchapter S firms, the result is a distribution of 23%, 6%, and 35% as the active owners in each sector. Dividing by the total of active owners as a share, a new distribution of active business owners across the three types can be derived: 36%, 9%, and 55%.

Table A-1. Industry Distribution of Non-Employer Businesses

Industry	Percentage of Returns
Services	56.1
Professional Services	14.2
Other Services	14.2
Administrative Services	8.6
Health Services	8.5
Construction	11.8
Trade	12.8
Finance, Insurance, and Real Estate	13.4
Finance	3.4
Real Estate	10.0

Source: U.S. Bureau of the Census, http://www.census.gov/econ/nonemployer/.

To use these new shares to adjust the numbers, consider as a rule of thumb that single owner firms are similar, so that the Subchapter S firms with one owner are treated as having a similar share of non-employer firms as proprietorships. According to the data on Subchapter S firms, about 65% of firms have only one shareholder, and given the number of shareholders, 37% of shareholders are single owner firms. Excluding partnerships and multi-owner subchapter S firms, 56% (36% plus 0.37 times 55%) of active firms would have a single owner. Taxing 56% of the difference between 21% and 5%, is 9%, suggesting that the 21% share accruing to active businesses should be reduced to 12% (21% minus 9%) to account for non-employer owners.

Table A-2. Industry Distribution of Sole Proprietorships, 2007

Industry	Percentage of Returns
Services	52.8
Professional Services	14.0
Other Services	10.4
Administrative Support Services	9.7
Health Services	8.7
Construction	12.6
Trade	12.0
Finance, Insurance, and Real Estate	9.2
Finance and Insurance	6.0
Real Estate	3.1

Source: IRS Statistics of Income, Individual Income Taxes, http://www.irs.gov/taxstats/indtaxstats/article/0,,id= 134481,00.html.

Table A-3. Industry Distribution of Partnerships and Partners

	Percentage of Partnerships	Percentage of Partners	Average Number of Partners
Finance, Insurance, and Real Estate	58.0	60.5	6.2
Finance and Insurance	48.1	36.6	4.6
Real Estate	9.9	23.8	14.3
Services	18.4	15.1	4.4
Professional	5.6	3.5	3.7
Food and Accommodations	3.4	2.0	3.6
Trade	7.1	4.6	3.7
Construction	6.7	3.0	2.7

Source: Tim Wheeler and Nina Shuofsky, "Partnership Returns 2007." Internal Revenue Service Statistics of Income Bulletin, Fall 2009, pp. 70-159, http://www.irs.gov/pub/irs-soi/09fallbulpartret.pdf.

Notes: For all industries, the average is six partners.

Table A-4. Industry Distribution of Subchapter S Firms and Shareholders, 200

	Percentage of Firms	Percentage of Shareholders	Average Number o of Shareholders
Services	41.6	38.7	1.6
Professional Services	15.3	12.9	1.5
Health and Social Services	6.2	5.1	1.4
Trade	16.9	16.8	1.7
Finance, Insurance, and Real Estate	15.1	17.0	1.9
Finance and Insurance	4.0	3.8	1.6
Real Estate	11.1	13.2	2.1
Construction	13.4	12.4	1.6

Source: Internal Revenue Service Statistics of Income, http://www.irs.gov/pub/irs-soi/03scorp.pdf.

Notes: Average Number of Shareholders for all firms is 1.8.

End Notes

[1]See U.S. Department of the Treasury, *General Explanations of the Administration's Fiscal Year 2011 Revenue Proposals*, February 2010, http://www.treas.gov/offices/tax-policy p. 152. The other proposals are to retain the phase-out of personal exemptions (PEP) and itemized deductions (Pease), to retain a 20% tax rate for capital gains, and to tax dividend income at 20%.

[2] Some of the issues discussed in this report are also discussed in CRS Report R41085, *Distribution of Small Business Ownership and Income by Individual Tax Rates and Selected Policy Issues* , by Gary Guenther.

[3] Internal Revenue Service, Statistics of Income, Integrated Business Data, http://www.irs.gov/ taxstats/bustaxstats/ article/0,,id=152029,00.html.

[4] Joint Committee on Taxation, Present Law And The President's Fiscal Year 2011 Budget Proposals Related To Selected Individual Income Tax Provisions Scheduled To Expire Under The Sunset Provisions Of The Economic Growth And Tax Relief Reconciliation Act Of 2001. JCX-36-10, July 12, 2010, p. 10, http://www.jct.gov/ publications.html?func=startdown&id=3691.

[5] Returns with passive income are 9.2 million (27.5 million minus 18.3 million) which is 33.5% of the total. Passive income is $176 billion ($938 billion minus $762 billion) which is 18.8% of the total.

[6] Note that the returns with any business income are smaller than the sum of returns with each type of operation. This result occurs because taxpayers may report more than one type of business income. This effect is particularly pronounced at high income levels. For the population as a

whole the sum of returns with each type of income is 9% larger than the total returns reporting business income; for taxpayers subject to the higher tax rates, the sum is 42% larger. Much of that effect may be due to passive income.

[7] That is, in calculating the share, only returns with positive income should be in the numerator, but returns with both positive income and losses should be included in the denominator.

[8] Note that the effects for the AMT are different when the tax rates are presumed to be increased, as in the Tax Policy Center, as compared to the 2008 data in the IRS statistics, because the higher rates would cause fewer taxpayers to fall into the AMT.

[9] Bureau of the Census, http://www2.census.gov/econ/susb/data/2007/us_naicssector_lfo_2007.xls.

[10] The share of business income falling into these high tax rate categories is also reported. However, that share does not appear relevant to the issue of encouraging small business employment, as there is no evidence that businesses owned by high income employees have more employees than those owned by lower income employees; indeed, there is evidence that there is not a difference (discussed subsequently in the section on effects of taxes on small businesses).

[11] Urban Brookings Tax Policy Center, Table T10-0186, http://taxpolicycenter.org/numbers/displayatab.cfm?DocID= 2783&topic2ID=60&topic3ID=68&DocTypeID=

[12] Data are from the Census Bureau. Data on businesses are at http://www.census.gov/econ/susb/. Data on non employers is at http://www.census.gov/econ/nonemployer/ and data on employers is at http://www2.census.gov/econ/ susb/data/2007/us_state_totals_2007.xls.

[13] As will be seen below, there is a single study on this issue; this evidence suggests an effect that would be small. See Robert Carroll, Douglas Holtz- Eakin, Mark Rider, and Harvey S. Rosen, "Income Taxes and Entrepreneurs' Use of Labor," *Journal of Labor Economics*, vol. 18, pp. 324-351.

[14] David Birch, "Who Creates Jobs?" *Public Interest*, V. 65, Fall 1981, pp. 3-14.

[15] Brian Headd, An Analysis of Small Business and Jobs, Small Business Administration Office of Advocacy, March 2010. http://www.sba.gov/advo/research/rs359tot.pdf.

[16] Catherine Armington and Marjorie Odle, "Small Business: How Many Jobs," *The Brookings Review*, V. 1, No.2, Winter 1982, pp. 104. John Case has argued that the Armington-Odle criticism is not correct but does not elaborate on the issue. See his book, *From the Ground Up: The Resurgence of American Entrepreneurship*, New York: Simon and Schuster, 1992 and his article, The Disciples of David Birch, in *INC*, January 1989, pp. 3945.

[17] Charles Brown, James Hamilton, and James Medoff, *Employers Large and Small*, Cambridge: Harvard University Press, 1990.

[18] Milton Friedman, "Do Old Fallacies Ever Die?" *Journal of Economic Literature*, Vol. 30, December 1992, pp. 2129-2132. Friedman began by describing a criticism of a study by Horace Secrist in 1933 where this fallacy of regression to the mean appears. He went on to say, in describing other studies where this problem arose: "For example, 'everyone knows' that job creation comes mainly from small firms. That proposition may be true but the evidence offered for it that I have seen classifies firms by size in an initial year and traces subsequent levels of employment— precisely what Secrist did. I have yet to see what the data show if firms are classified by their terminal size, or by their average size over a period." (p. 2131).

[19] Steven J. Davis, John C. Haltiwanger, and Scott Schuh, *Job Creation and Destruction*, MIT Press, Cambridge MA 1996.

[20] David Neumark, Brandon Wall and Junfu Zhang, "Do Small Businesses Create more Jobs? New Evidence from National Establishment Time Series." National Bureau of Economic Research Working Paper, 13818, Cambridge, MA, February 2008.

[21] John Haltiwanger, Ron S Jarmin, and Javier Miranda, "Who Creates Jobs? Small vs. Large vs. Young" National Bureau of Economic Research working Paper 16300, Cambridge, MA, August 2010.

[22] Brian Headd, An Analysis of Small Business and Jobs, Small Business Administration Office of Advocacy, March 2010. http://www.sba.gov/advo/research/rs359tot.pdf.

[23] See CRS Report R40860, *Defining Small Business: An Historical Analysis of Contemporary Issues*, by Robert Jay Dilger.

[24] Charles Brown, James Hamilton, and James Medoff, *Employers Large and Small*, Cambridge: Harvard University Press, 1990.

[25] Steven J. Davis, John C. Haltiwanger, and Scott Schuh, *Job Creation and Destruction*, MIT Press, Cambridge MA 1996.

[26] Brian Headd, An Analysis of Small Business and Jobs, Small Business Administration Office of Advocacy, March 2010. http://www.sba.gov/advo/research/rs359tot.pdf.

[27] Herbert J. Schuetze and Donald Bruce, "Tax Policy and Entrepreneurship," *Swedish Economic Policy Review*, vol. 11, 2004, pp. 233-263, http://www.sweden. gov.se/ content/1/c6/09/ 54/27/848f6cf1.pdf.

[28] Thomas A. Garrett and Howard H. Wall, "Creating a Policy Environment for Entrepreneurs," Federal Reserve Board of St/ Louis, Working Paper 2005-064B, revised March 2006, http://research.stlouisfed.org/wp/2005/2005-064.pdf.

[29] Donald Bruce and John Deskins, "State Tax Policy and Entrepreneurial Activity," Small Business Administration Office of Advocacy, November 2006. http://www.sba.gov/advo/ research/rs284tot.pdf.

[30] Donald Bruce and Mohammed Mohsin, "Tax Policy and Entrepreneurship: New Time Series Evidence," *Small Business Economics*, vol. 26, Spring 2006, pp. 409-4245, http://www. springerlink.com/content/v56w50731587m752/fulltext.pdf.

[31] Tami Gurley-Calvez and Donald Bruce, "Do Tax Cuts Prolong Entrepreneurial Longevity?" *National Tax Journal* vol. 61, June 2008, pp. 225-249.

[32] See CRS Report R40219, *Tax Gap, Tax Enforcement, and Tax Compliance Proposals in the 111th Congress*, by James M. Bickley, for data indicating tax gap estimates that show significant underreporting by unincorporated businesses compared to underreporting of wages.

[33] Under proportional taxation and full loss offset, the effect of this reduction in risk can fully offset the effect of the tax on the expected earnings, as taxpayers can increase the share of risky assets in their portfolio to achieve the original no-tax solution. See Evsey Domar and Richard Musgrave, "Proportional Income Taxation, and Risk Taking," *Quarterly Journal of Economics*, vol. 58, May 1944, pp. 388-342. Progressive rates and limits on losses reduce, but do not eliminate, the value of this risk reduction.

[34] Three papers were published on the basis of this study. See Robert Carroll, Douglas Holtz- Eakin, Mark Rider, and Harvey S. Rosen, "Entrepreneurs, Income Taxes and Investments, in *Does Atlas Shrug? The Economic Consequences of Taxing the Rich*, ed. Joel Slemrod, Russell Sage Foundation, New York, 2000; Income Taxes and Entrepreneurs' Use of Labor," *Journal of Labor Economics*, vol. 18, pp. 324-351; "Personal Income Taxes and the Growth of Small Firms, in Tax Policy and the Economy 15," ed. James Poterba, MIT Press, Cambridge, MA, 2001.

[35] The study reports an elasticity (percentage change in quantity divided by percentage change in price) of the probability of hiring workers relative to the net of tax share (1-t) of 1.2 and elasticity of the wage bill conditional on having workers as 0.37. The tax price of those in the top bracket would increase by 7.8% (1-0.35)/(1-.0396) and the tax price of those in the second highest bracket would increase by 4.7% (1-.33)/(1-.36). Weighting those effects by the share of

firms in each group in Table 3 yields a weighted change of 6.8%. The share of firms with workers in their data set is 0.21, so the percentage increase in employment is 0.068 times 0.21 times 1.2 times 0.036, the last number being the share of firms affected. The percentage increase in wages (and possibly employment) would be 0.068 times 0.37 times 0.36.

[36] For this effect, the elasticity (percentage change in the probability of hiring workers divided by the percentage change in net of tax share (or 1-t, where t is the tax rate) is 1.2 and for wages paid conditional on having employees 0.37 which would be considered large even for own labor supply response. For a review of labor supply responses see CRS Report RL31949, *Issues in Dynamic Revenue Estimating*, by Jane G. Gravelle; for a study finding virtually no effect of taxes on hours by the affluent, see Riobert A. Moffitt and Mark O. Wilhelm, "Taxation and Labor Supply Decisions of the Affluent in *Does Atlas Shrug? The Economic Consequences of Taxing the Rich*, ed. Joel Slemrod, Russell Sage Foundation, New York, 2000.

[37] This approach compares the change in behavior of low tax and high tax individuals. One of the reservations with this type of approach is that these taxpayers may differ systematically in their growth rates in the absence of change and their response to tax rates. Examining a period when tax rates rose, such as 1993, would help to determine if this problem existed. For a discussion see CRS Report RL33672, *Revenue Feedback from the 2001-2004 Tax Cuts*, by Jane G. Gravelle, and Emmanuel Saez, Joel B. Slemrod, and Seth H. Giertz, "The Elasticity of Taxable Income with Respect to Marginal Tax Rates: A Critical Review," NBER Working Paper 15012, Cambridge, MA, May 2009, http://elsa.berkeley.edu/~saez/saez-slemrod-giertzNBER09.pdf.

[38] To use an example of market adjustment, during the 20th century there was a massive contraction in the share of employment in agriculture and accompanying growth in other types of employment. This shift in employment shares did not, however, mean that agriculture was less efficient. Indeed, it was the consequence of enormous technological progress in agriculture, through mechanization and other technical advances, that allowed fewer labor resources to be devoted to farming.

[39] Several CRS Reports discuss these issues. See CRS Report R40104, *Economic Stimulus: Issues and Policies*, by Jane G. Gravelle, Thomas L. Hungerford, and Marc Labonte; CRS Report RS21136, *Government Spending or Tax Reduction: Which Might Add More Stimulus to the Economy?* by Marc Labonte; CRS Report R41034, *Business Investment and Employment Tax Incentives to Stimulate the Economy*, by Thomas L. Hungerford and Jane G. Gravelle; CRS Report RS21126, *Tax Cuts and Economic Stimulus: How Effective Are the Alternatives?*, by Jane G. Gravelle; CRS Report R41006, *Unemployment: Issues and Policies*, by Jane G. Gravelle, Thomas L. Hungerford, and Marc Labonte

[40] Brian Headd, An Analysis of Small Business and Jobs, Small Business Administration Office of Advocacy, March 2010. http://www.sba.gov/advo/research/rs359tot.pdf.

[41] See Jane G. Gravelle, "Federal Taxation of Small Business: How Favorable? How Justified?" http://www.ntanet.org/images and Eric Toder, "Does the Federal Income Tax Favor Small Business?" http://www.ntanet.org/images/stories/ pdf/ proceedings/07/018.pdf, both in *the 2007 Proceedings of the National Tax Association*, and CRS Report RL32254, *Small Business Tax Benefits: Overview of Current Law and Economic Justification*, by Gary Guenther.

[42] Because one source of capital income, active investment income of Subchapter S firms is excluded from the Medicare tax, the Medicare tax will become a benefit rather than a penalty for small business.

[43] Douglas Holtz-Eakin, "Should Small Business be Tax Favored?" *National Tax Journal*, vol. 48. September 1995, pp. 387-395; Kelly Edmiston, "The Role of Small and Large Businesses in Economic Development," Federal Reserve Bank of Kansas City, *Economic Review*, 2nd Quarter, 2007, http://www.kc.frb.org/PUBLICAT/ECONREV/PDF/2q07edmi.pdf.

[44] Robert Carroll, Douglas Holtz- Eakin, Mark Rider, and Harvey S. Rosen, "Income Taxes and Entrepreneurs' Use of Labor," *Journal of Labor Economics*, vol. 18, pp. 324-351.

In: Federal Taxation
Editor: Jaclyn N. Prichard

ISBN: 978-1-61324-102-8

Chapter 5

THE ECONOMIC EFFECTS OF CAPITAL GAINS TAXATION*

Thomas L. Hungerford

SUMMARY

One provision of the 1913 individual income tax that generated a great deal of confusion was the taxation of income from the sale of property (i.e., capital gains income). This initial confusion has led to almost 100 years of legislative debates over capital gains. Beginning in 1922 capital gains were first subject to lower tax rates than ordinary income. This preferential treatment has continued throughout most of the history of the income tax. Proposals dealing with the taxation of capital gains have ranged from the outright elimination of capital gains taxation to the reduction of capital gains tax rates for certain classes of taxpayers to the elimination of the preferential tax treatment.

Overall, capital gains tax revenues have been a fairly small, but not trivial, source of government revenue. Since 1954, revenue from the capital gains tax as a share of total income tax revenue has averaged 5.2%. It reached a peak of 12.8% in 1986 and a low of 2.0% in 1957. Nonetheless, the 2007 capital gains tax revenue of $123 billion was equal to 75% of the FY2007 budget deficit.

Some argue that reducing capital gains tax rates will increase tax revenues by dramatically increasing capital gains realizations. While the

---

* This is an edited, reformatted and augmented version of Congressional Research Services publication R40411, dated June 18, 2010.

effect of changes in the capital gains tax rate continue to be debated and researched, the bulk of the evidence suggests that reducing the capital gains tax rate reduces tax revenues.

Higher income households are substantially more likely to own assets that can generate taxable gains than lower income households. Additionally, high income households own most of these assets, realize most of the capital gains, and pay most of the capital gains taxes at preferential rates.

Capital gains tax reductions are often proposed as a policy that will increase saving and investment, provide a short-term economic stimulus, and boost long-term economic growth. Capital gains tax rate reductions appear to decrease public saving and may have little or no effect on private saving. Consequently, many analysts note that capital gains tax reductions likely have a negative overall impact on national saving. Furthermore, capital gains tax rate reductions, they observe, are unlikely to have much effect on the long-term level of output or the path to the long-run level of output (i.e., economic growth). A tax reduction on capital gains would mostly benefit very high income taxpayers who are likely to save most of any tax reduction. A temporary capital gains tax reduction possibly could have a negative impact on short-term economic growth.

INTRODUCTION

One provision of the 1913 individual income tax that generated a great deal of confusion was the taxation of income from the sale of property (i.e., capital gains income). This initial confusion has led to almost 100 years of legislative debates over capital gains. For the first nine years of the individual income tax, capital gains received no preferential treatment and were taxed as ordinary income. Beginning in 1922, however, capital gains were first subject to lower tax rates than ordinary income. This preferential treatment has continued throughout most of the history of the income tax.

Proposals and legislation dealing with the taxation of capital gains have ranged from the outright elimination of capital gains taxation to the reduction of capital gains tax rates for certain classes of taxpayers to the elimination of the preferential tax treatment. For example, the American Recovery and Reinvestment Act of 2009 (ARRA; P.L. 111-5) increased the exclusion of capital gains from the sale of certain small business stock held for more than five years from 50% to 75%.

HOW CAPITAL GAINS ARE TAXED

Proposals to deal with how capital gains are taxed depend on how capital gains are defined. Under the Haig-Simons approach, income is defined as consumption plus the change in wealth.[1] Wealth can increase because of active saving or because the value of assets has increased; capital gains are the increase in the value of capital assets. Under this income definition, real or inflation-adjusted capital gains would be taxed each year as they accrue and real capital losses would be deducted. It has long been recognized, however, that taxing real capital gains as they accrue may be impractical especially for capital assets that are not actively traded.

Given the difficulties of taxing capital gains as they accrue, capital gains are taxed as they are realized (that is, when the capital asset is sold or exchanged). Capital assets are property, but there are exceptions such as business inventory, accounts receivable acquired in the ordinary course of business, copyrights, and literary compositions.[2] Capital gains are calculated by subtracting the asset's basis from the sales price. An asset's basis is the original purchase price adjusted for certain additions and deductions; it is not adjusted for inflation. If the basis is greater than the sales price then it is a capital loss.

Capital gains are taxed at various rates. For the 2008 tax year, short-term capital gains (gains on capital assets held for less than one year) are taxed as ordinary income. Long-term capital gains are taxed at a 0% tax rate for taxpayers in the two lowest tax brackets (the 10% and 15% tax brackets) and at 15% for other taxpayers. Capital gains and capital losses are treated asymmetrically. Capital losses are subtracted from capital gains before calculating tax liability. If capital losses exceed capital gains, then up to $3,000 of capital losses can be deducted from ordinary income. Capital losses in excess of $3,000 can be carried over and subtracted from income in future years.[3]

CAPITAL GAINS TAX RATES AND TAX REVENUES

Both capital gains tax rates and tax revenues have constantly changed since the establishment of the income tax. Tax revenues depend on the tax rate and capital gains realizations. Capital gains realizations, in turn, depend on tax rates as well as other factors.

Tax Rates

Throughout most of the history of the income tax, the maximum capital gains tax rate has been lower than the maximum tax rate on ordinary income. Figure 1 displays the capital gains and ordinary income tax rates for the past 50 years. With the exception of a three-year period (1988- 1990), the capital gains tax rate was considerably below the tax rate for ordinary income. After 2010, the capital gains tax rate is scheduled to revert back to 20%. The 15% maximum capital gains tax rate between 2003 and 2010 is the lowest rate on long-term capital gains since the Second World War.

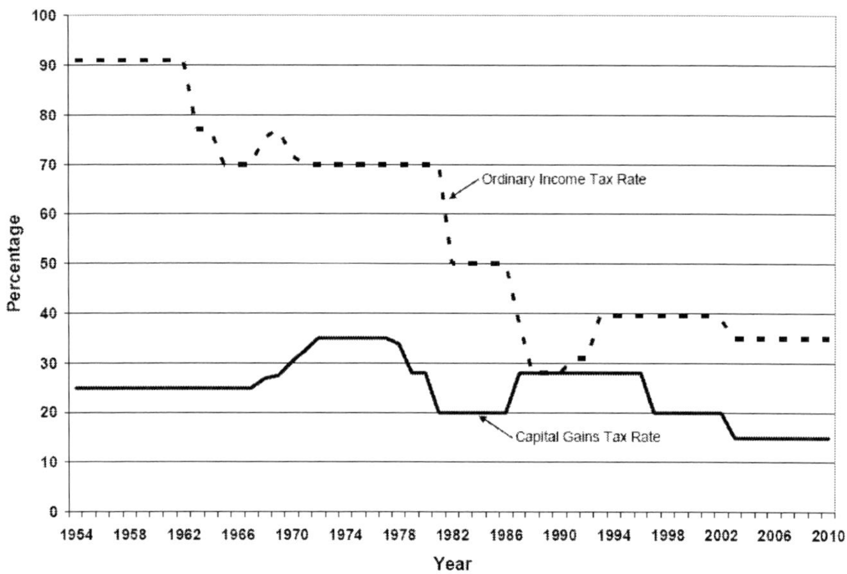

Source: Department of the Treasury.

Figure 1. Maximum Tax Rates on Capital Gains and Ordinary Income, 1954-2010.

Tax Revenues

Overall, capital gains tax revenues have been a fairly small, but not trivial, source of government revenue. Since 1954, revenue from the capital gains tax as a share of total income tax revenue has averaged 5.2%. It reached a peak of 12.8% in 1986 and a low of 2.0% in 1957. Nonetheless, the 2007 capital gains tax revenue of $123 billion was equal to 75% of the FY2007 budget deficit.

Capital gains tax revenue generally follows the same trend as capital gains realizations. Figure 2 shows both as a percentage of gross domestic product (GDP) from 1954 to 2008 along with CBO projections to 2019. Realizations and revenues hit peaks in 1986, 2000, and 2007.

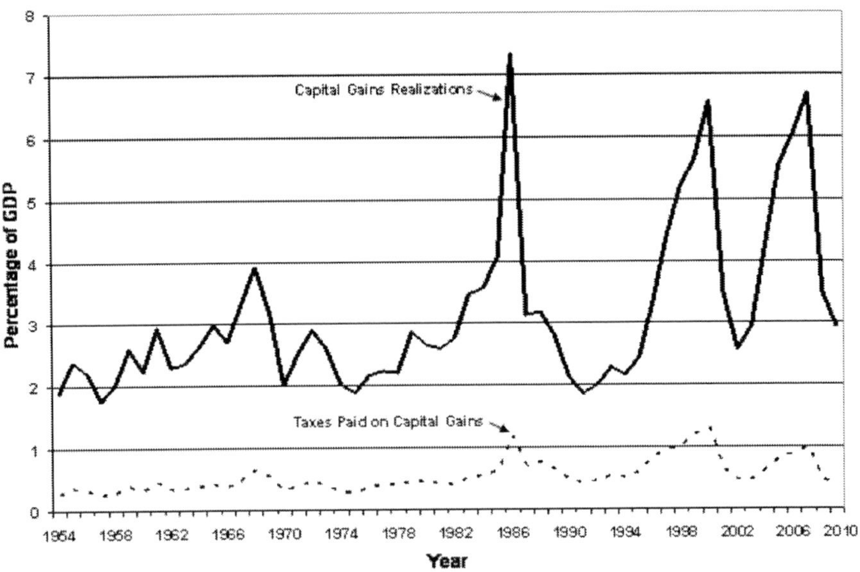

Figure 2. Capital Gains Realizations and Tax Revenue, 1954-2010; (As a percentage of GDP) Source: Department of the Treasury and CBO.

Behavioral Responses to Capital Gains Tax Rate Changes

The capital gains tax discourages capital gains realizations because capital gains are only taxed when realized. Consequently, taxpayers tend to hold on to appreciated assets they would otherwise sell. Furthermore, step-up in basis at death gives taxpayers an incentive to hold assets until death and pass them to their heirs. In these ways, the capital gains tax is said to produce a "lock-in" effect. This effect imposes efficiency losses because investors may be encouraged to hold suboptimal portfolios or forego investment opportunities with higher pre-tax returns. Changes in the capital gains tax rate can exacerbate or reduce lock-in effects, and thus affect realizations and tax revenues.

Changes in the capital gains tax rate tend to track capital gains realizations. Figure 3 shows the maximum capital gains tax rate and capital gains realizations as a percentage of GDP. The major spikes in realizations correspond to changes in the tax rate. The simple correlation between the two time-series is -0.64, which suggests that realizations increase when the tax rate decreases. It is this relationship that has led some to argue that decreasing the capital gains tax rate will increase capital gains tax revenues.

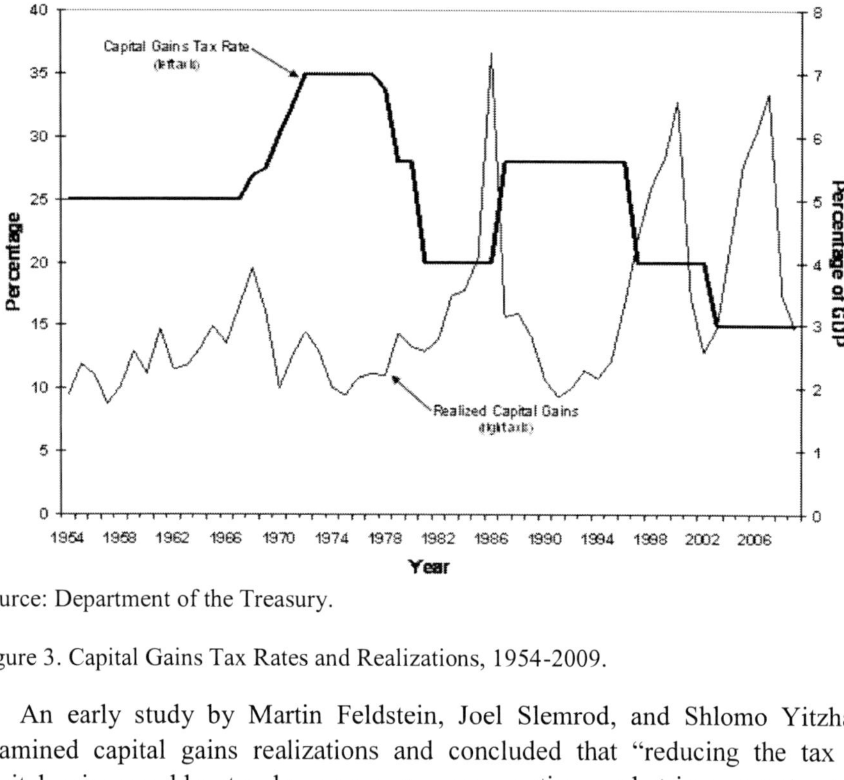

Source: Department of the Treasury.

Figure 3. Capital Gains Tax Rates and Realizations, 1954-2009.

An early study by Martin Feldstein, Joel Slemrod, and Shlomo Yitzhaki examined capital gains realizations and concluded that "reducing the tax on capital gains would not only encourage a more active market in corporate stock but would also increase tax revenue."[4] Their estimated elasticity was about 3.8, suggesting that a 10% reduction in the tax rate would increase realizations by 38%. This estimate was criticized because it used data from only one year—1973.[5] This cross-sectional evidence was likely picking up a temporary timing response in realizations from the tax rate change rather than a behavioral response to a permanent change in the tax rate.[6]

Some analysts have argued that a large permanent response to capital gains tax rate changes is implausible. Alan Auerbach has suggested that there is nothing in the historical record of capital gains to justify a large elasticity.[7] Jane Gravelle points out that capital gains realizations cannot be greater than accruals. Her simulation model suggests an upper limit for the permanent realization elasticity is 0.5.[8]

Empirical research has tried to separate the transitory response from the permanent response. Gerald Auten and Charles Clotfelter used panel data, a dataset containing observations on individuals over a period of years (1969 to 1973), to estimate the temporary and permanent effects of a capital gains tax cut.[9] They estimate a transitory elasticity that is generally greater than 1.0 (the simple average from all their specifications is 1.5) suggesting that a 10% reduction in the tax rate would lead to a 15% increase in short-run realizations (the timing response). The permanent or long-run elasticity they estimated was 0.5.

In subsequent research, Leonard Burman and William Randolph estimate a permanent elasticity that is closer to zero than to 0.5.[10] They, however, report a large transitory elasticity of 6.4. A large transitory elasticity and a low permanent elasticity are consistent with the pattern of capital gains realizations shown in Figure 3. Changes in the tax rate or anticipated changes have coincided with large increases in capital gains realizations, but realizations quickly fell back to previous levels. The spike in 1986 was due to the transitory response to the announced increase in the capital gains tax rate to take effect in 1987. The spikes in 2000 and 2007 were the transitory responses to capital gains tax rate reductions.

Over the years, a variety of studies have estimated different long-run or permanent realizations elasticities. The general trend has been to estimate elasticities closer to zero than to 1.0 as data and estimation methods improve, though there are exceptions. However, even an elasticity of 1.0 does not mean that reducing the capital gains tax rate is revenue neutral. Taxpayers may increase their capital gains realizations by shifting other income into capital gains. This may increase capital gains tax revenue, but will reduce tax revenues from other sources—overall, tax revenues fall. While the effect of changes in the capital gains tax rate continue to be debated and researched, the bulk of the evidence suggests that reducing the capital gains tax rate reduces tax revenues.

DISTRIBUTIONAL ISSUES

Three questions can be asked about distributional issues related to capital gains: (1) who owns the assets that can generate capital gains? (2) who realizes capital gains? and (3) who pays capital gains taxes? Each question is examined. Two data sources are used for the analysis: the Federal Reserve Board's 2007 Survey of Consumer Finances (SCF) and the IRS's 2004 Statistics of Income

Public Use File (SOI PUF). See the Appendix for a description of each data source.

Assets and Accrued Capital Gains

Most assets owned by households would not be subject to capital gains taxes when sold. Figure 4 reports the various assets that households owned in 2007. Over half of the total is accounted for by retirement accounts (e.g., 401(k)s and IRAs) and principal residences. Retirement accounts generally are not taxed until the funds are withdrawn at retirement. At that time, the withdrawals are taxed as ordinary income. Up to $500,000 of the gain from the sale of a principal residence can be excluded from income taxes. Farm and business assets and other real estate (e.g., rental property, and vacation homes) account for 33% of household assets. The final 13% of household assets are financial assets (i.e., stocks, bonds, and mutual funds).

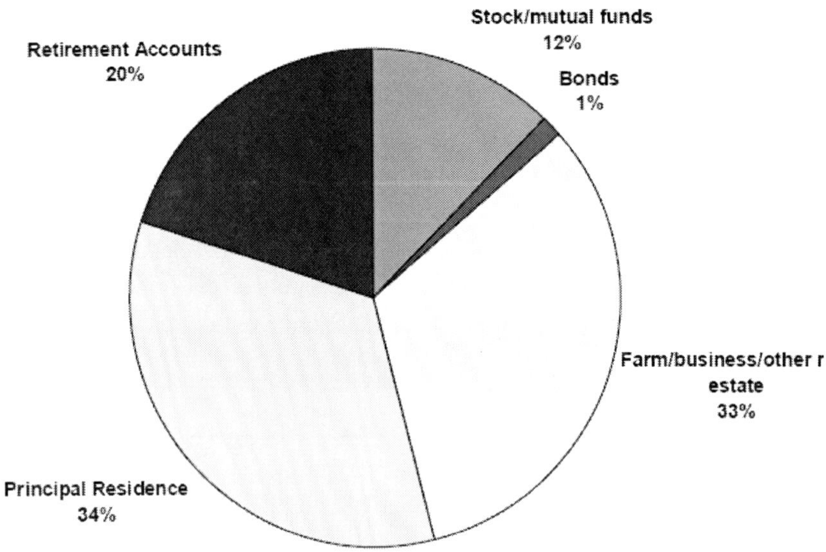

Source: CRS analysis of the 2007 SCF.

Figure 4. Assets Owned by Households, 2007.

Higher income households are more likely to own assets that can generate taxable capital gains than lower income households. Table 1 reports the proportion of households in each income category owning particular assets. For each type of asset, the proportion owning increases as income increases. For example, 7% of the poorest 20% of households own stocks or mutual funds compared to 72% of the richest 5% of households.

Table 1. Percentage Owning Assets by Income, 2007

Income category	Stocks/mutual funds	Bonds	Farm, business, other	Principal residence	Retirement accounts
Quintile 1	6.9%	0.3%	10.0%	40.5%	11.2%
Quintile 2	11.5	0.2	13.5	57.1	34.6
Quintile 3	20.5	1.1	24.2	72.5	56.9
Quintile 4	30.4	1.2	31.0	82.6	73.6
Quintile 5	52.2	5.4	51.7	90.7	87.1
Top 10%	59.9	9.3	64.6	92.6	89.8
Top 5%	71.9	13.7	75.7	93.8	91.4

Source: CRS analysis of the 2007 SCF.

Most of the assets are owned by higher income households. Well over half of the assets that can generate taxable capital gains are owned by the richest 5% of households (see **Table 2**). Principal residences are more broadly distributed in the income distribution than other assets, but most of the gains from the sale of homes is excluded from federal taxation.

Table 2. Distribution of Assets by Income, 2007

Income category	Stocks/mutual funds	Bonds	Farm, business, other	Principal residence	Retirement Accounts
Quintile 1	1.0%	0.7%	3.1%	4.9%	0.4%
Quintile 2	1.5	0.2	3.0	9.1	2.4
Quintile 3	4.2	2.0	5.1	15.0	7.0
Quintile 4	10.2	3.8	9.5	22.0	20.4
Quintile 5	83.0	93.3	79.2	49.1	69.8
Top 10%	75.9	89.5	71.3	33.1	51.3
Top 5%	66.4	85.5	60.8	22.3	37.4

Source: CRS analysis of the 2007 SCF.

The distribution of capital accruals tends to follow the same pattern as the distribution of asset ownership. Table 3 reports the distribution of accrued capital gains for selected assets.[11] Capital gains accruals for stocks, mutual funds, and businesses are highly skewed toward the upper income levels. About 90% of capital gains accruals go to households in the richest income quintile and 70% go to the richest 5% of households. Capital gains accruals on principal residences, however, are less skewed—only 47% go to households in the richest income quintile.

Table 3. Accrued Capital Gains by Income, 2007

Income category	Stocks/mutual funds	Businesses	Other real estate	Principal residences
Quintile 1	0.7%	1.8%	3.3%	5.5%
Quintile 2	0.6	2.0	4.1	9.9
Quintile 3	1.5	2.8	8.2	16.0
Quintile 4	7.0	5.6	14.0	21.2
Quintile 5	90.2	87.8	70.4	47.4
Top 10%	85.4	80.6	60.0	31.6
Top 5%	75.7	69.2	49.4	20.9

Source: CRS analysis of the 2007 SCF.

Capital Gains Realizations and Taxes

The distribution of realized capital gains can be examined by one of two methods. First, the focus can be on how capital gains are distributed among all households. This allows for an examination of how income from capital gains is distributed throughout the entire income distribution.

Second, the focus can be narrowed to examine how realized capital gains are distributed among taxpayers—the group that reports income from capital gains. Many lower income individuals and families, such as those with income primarily from public assistance or Social Security, do not file tax returns and would be excluded from the analysis. Both methods are employed.

Income from realized capital gains, while always concentrated at the top of the income distribution, has become more concentrated over the past 25 years. Figure 5 displays the distribution of realized capital gains among all households (whether or not they filed tax returns) since 1979. In 1979, households in the bottom 95% of the income distribution received about 20% of total capital gains income (the dark grey and white bars). The richest 0.1% of households (about 81,000 households) received 36% of total capital gains income. By 2005, the bottom 95% received only 10% of total capital gains income while the richest 0.1% (about 114,000 households) received 50%.

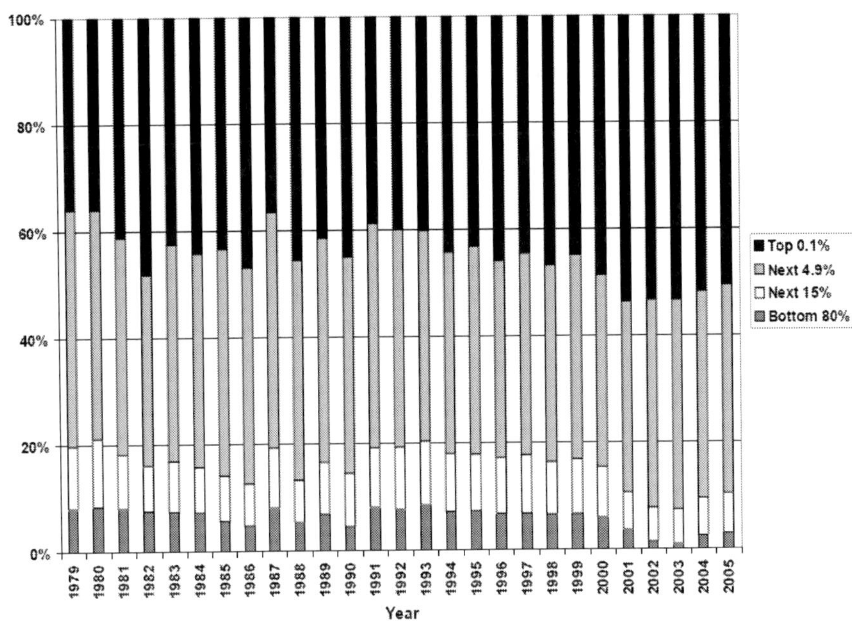

Source: CBO, Historical Effective Tax Rates, 1979-2005: Supplement, December 2008.

Figure 5. Distribution of Realized Capital Gains by Income, 1979-2005.

Income from realized capital gains is only slightly more broadly distributed among taxpayers. Table 4 reports the distribution of long-term capital gains and all capital gains in 2004. Longterm capital gains are taxed at preferential rates while short-term capital gains are not. About 18% of total long-term capital gains were received by taxpayers in the bottom 80% of the income distribution. Taxpayers in the top 20% received about 82% of total long-term capital gains and taxpayers in the richest 5% received 68% of total capital gains in 2004.

Table 4. Capital Gains Income and Capital Gains Taxes, 2004

Income category	Long-term capital gains	All capital gains	Taxes paid on capital gains
Quintile 1	2.7%	2.8%	1.4%
Quintile 2	3.3	3.5	2.1
Quintile 3	5.2	5.4	3.7
Quintile 4	6.9	7.0	6.1
Quintile 5	81.9	81.3	86.7
Top 10%	74.6	74.2	79.2
Top 5%	68.2	67.5	71.7

Source: 2004 IRS SOI PUF.

The final column of Table 4 reports the distribution of capital gains taxes (on both short-term and long-term capital gains). Overall, the distributional pattern is similar to the capital gains income distribution, but slightly more skewed toward the higher income levels. The primary reason is that lower income taxpayers faced a 5% long-term capital gains tax rate in 2004 while higher income taxpayers faced a 15% tax rate.

ECONOMIC ISSUES

Capital gains tax reductions are often proposed as a policy that will increase saving and investment, provide a short-term economic stimulus, and boost long-term economic growth. Each of these arguments is examined.

Saving and Investment

National saving is made up of saving by the government (public saving) and by households and firms (private saving). Public saving is equal to the government's deficit or surplus—it is negative for a deficit and positive for a surplus. Reducing capital gains tax rates will likely reduce public saving because it reduces tax revenues without affecting outlays; this increases a budget deficit or decreases a budget surplus.[12]

Households save by investing in their own business or investing in stocks, bonds, and other financial instruments. Changing capital gains tax rates changes the after-tax rate of return on investments (for example, reducing the tax rate increases the after-tax return). The change in the rate of return has two offsetting effects on saving. Increasing the rate of return can increase households' willingness to save (the substitution effect). But at the same time, the increased return allows households to save less to maintain their desired or target wealth level (the income effect). Consequently, the effect of capital gains taxes on private saving is likely to be small.

The traditional economic theory of saving, the life-cycle model, assumes that individuals make rational, far-sighted decisions. The preponderance of empirical evidence, however, does not support the life-cycle model.[13] Behavioral theories of saving emphasize the role of inertia, the lack of self-control, and the limit of human intellectual capabilities. To cope with the complexities involved in making saving decisions, individuals often use simple rules of thumb and develop target levels of wealth. Once their target level of wealth is obtained, many individuals suspend active saving.[14] Saving rates have fallen over the past 30 years while the capital gains tax rate has fallen from 28% in 1987 to 15% today (0% for taxpayers in the 10% and 15% tax brackets). This suggests that changing capital gains tax rates have had little effect on private saving.

Some have argued that preferential capital gains tax rates will boost high risk investments such as in venture capital. Most venture capital, however, is supplied by pension funds, college endowments, foundations, and insurance companies—sources not associated with the capital gains tax. In 2003, only about 10% of investors in venture capital funds were individuals and families.[15]

Additionally, for risk adverse investors, the capital gains tax could act as an insurance for risky investments by reducing losses as well as gains—it decreases the variability of returns.[16] The $3,000 loss limit may reduce the insurance value of the capital gains tax. But research has shown that almost three-quarters of taxpayers with capital losses were not subject to the loss limit because losses were less than $3,000 or gains offset the losses.[17] Of those affected by the loss limit, two-thirds were able to deduct losses against gains or other income within two years. The capital gains tax, therefore, may have little effect on risk-taking and may even encourage it.

Capital gains tax rate reductions appear to decrease public saving and may have little or no effect on private saving. Consequently, capital gains tax reductions likely have a negative overall impact on national saving.

Economic Growth

Some have argued that reducing capital gains tax rates would increase short-run and long-run economic growth.[18] The long-run level of output depends on the amount of saving and investment. Saving and investment increase the amount of capital in the economy and hence, aggregate supply (i.e., the amount of goods and services available in the economy). Many economists note that capital gains tax reductions appear to have little or even a negative effect on saving and investment (see above). Consequently, capital gains tax rate reductions are unlikely to have much effect on the long-term level of output or the path to the long-run level of output (i.e., economic growth).

Furthermore, it is argued that a temporary or permanent capital gains tax reduction is an effective economic stimulus measure. An effective short-term economic stimulus, however, will have to increase aggregate demand, which requires additional spending. A tax reduction on capital gains would mostly benefit very high income taxpayers who are likely to save most of any tax reduction.[19] Economists note that a temporary capital gains tax reduction possibly could have a negative impact on short-term economic growth. A temporary tax cut could induce investors to sell stock (i.e., realize capital gains by reducing the lock-in effect), but provides no incentive to invest since investors know they will face higher tax rates in the future. To the extent that the resulting sell-off depresses stock prices, consumer confidence, already low during recessions, could be further undermined thus reducing consumer spending.

A permanent capital gains tax cut will likely have two offsetting effects on stock prices. There is the demand-side capitalization effect—investors would be willing to pay a higher price for assets on which they would pay lower capital gains taxes in the future (in essence shifting out the demand curve). But there is also the supply-side lock-in effect in which investors would be willing to sell at a lower price because they have to pay lower capital gains taxes (in essence shifting out the supply curve). The ultimate effect on stock returns depends on the relative magnitude of these two effects, but it would likely be small in either direction.

Appendix. Data Sources

Two data sources are used in the analysis. The first is the 2007 Survey of Consumer Finances (SCF), which is prepared by the Federal Reserve Board. The SCF includes detailed information on household demographics, income, and wealth. In the analysis, households are ranked in the income distribution and assigned to income categories (quintiles) by their equivalence-adjusted household income, which is household income divided by the square root of family size. Each income quintile contains 20% of the households; in addition, the richest 10% (decile) and richest 5% (ventile) are included in the analysis. This adjustment controls for economies of scale within the household. Household income consists of income from all sources including public assistance, but excludes capital gains. All households are represented in the SCF sample regardless of whether or not they paid taxes.

Some analysts argue that capital gains income can temporarily make a low or moderate income household appear rich. To the extent that this is true, most capital gains income will appear to be received solely by the rich. Consequently, capital gains income is excluded from household income when assigning households to income categories. Most individuals and families, however, are in the same income category regardless of capital gains income—92% remain in the same quintile and 77% remain in the same ventile.

The second data source is the IRS's 2004 Statistics of Income Public Use File (SOI PUF). The SOI PUF contains information from the tax returns of a representative sample of taxpayers. Individuals and families that do not file a tax return are not included in this data source. These individuals and families are not required to file a tax return because of low income or receive primarily nontaxable income (e.g., public assistance). Taxpayers are assigned to income categories based on equivalence-adjusted total income; total income excludes capital gains income.

End Notes

[1] See Henry C. Simons, *Personal Income Taxation* (Chicago: University of Chicago Press, 1938).

[2] Capital assets are defined in Section 1221 of the Internal Revenue Code and explained in IRS publication 544. IRS publication 544 (p. 19) simply states that "[a]lmost everything you own and use for personal purposes or investment is a capital asset."

[3] See CRS Report RL31562, *An Analysis of the Tax Treatment of Capital Losses*, by Thomas L. Hungerford and Jane G. Gravelle.

[4] Martin Feldstein, Joel Slemrod, and Shlomo Yitzhaki, "The Effects of Taxation on the Selling of Corporate Stock and the Realizations of Capital Gains," *Quarterly Journal of Economics*, vol. 94, no. 4 (June 1980), p. 790.

[5] The authors note the problem of using cross-sectional data: "An individual whose tax rate varies substantially from year to year will tend to sell more when his rate is low. To the extent that low rates in 1973 are only temporarily low, our estimates will overstate the sensitivity of selling to the tax rate. We have no way of knowing how important this is" (p. 785).

[6] See Leonard E. Burman, *Labyrinth of Capital Gains Tax Policy: A Guide for the Perplexed* (Washington: Brookings Institution Press, 1999) and Jane G. Gravelle, *The Economic Effects of Taxing Capital Income* (Cambridge, MA: MIT Press, 1994) for discussions of this issue.

[7] Alan J. Auerbach, "Capital Gains Taxation and Tax Reform," *National Tax Journal*, vol. 42, no. 3 (1989), pp. 391-401. Auerbach concludes that "a permanent revenue increase [from a capital gains tax rate reduction] is unlikely enough to be discarded as a reason for reducing the capital gains tax rate" (p. 391).

[8] Jane G. Gravelle, "Limits to Capital Gains Feedback Effects," *Tax Notes*, vol. 51 (April 22, 1991), pp. 363-371.

[9] Gerald E. Auten and Charles T. Clotfelter, "Permanent versus Transitory Tax Effects and the Realization of Capital Gains," *Quarterly Journal of Economics*, vol. 97, no. 4 (November 1982), pp. 613-632.

[10] Leonard E. Burman and William C. Randolph, "Measuring Permanent Responses to Capital-Gains Tax Changes in Panel Data," *American Economic Review*, vol. 84, no. 4 (September 1994), pp. 794-809.

[11] The 2007 SCF doesn't allow capital gains accruals for other assets to be calculated.

[12] See Jane G. Gravelle, "Can A Capital Gains Tax Cut Pay for Itself," *Tax Notes*, vol. 48 (July 9, 1990), pp. 209-219.

[13] For a discussion and citations to the literature see CRS Report RL33482, *Saving Incentives: What May Work, What May Not*, by Thomas L. Hungerford.

[14] F. Thomas Juster, Joseph P. Lupton, James P. Smith, and Frank Stafford, "The Decline in Household Saving and the Wealth Effect," *Review of Economics and Statistics*, vol. 87, no. 4 (November 2005), pp. 20-27.

[15] National Venture Capital Association, *Venture Impact*, 4th Edition, 2007, available at http://www.nvca.org/pdf/ NVCA_VentureCapital07-2nd.pdf.

[16] See Burman, *Labyrinth of Capital Gains Tax Policy*.

[17] Alan J. Auerbach, Leonard E. Burman, and Jonathan M. Siegel, "Capital Gains Taxation and Tax Avoidance: New Evidence from Panel Data," in *Does Atlas Shrug?* ed. Joel B. Slemrod (Cambridge, MA: Harvard University Press, 2000), pp. 355-388.

[18] See, for example, Karen A. Campbell and Guinevere Nell, *Sustainable Economic Stimulus: Repeal Capital Gains and Dividend Taxes*, The Heritage Foundation, Web Memo no. 2263, February 3, 2009.

[19] See Jonathan McCarthy, "Imperfect Insurance and Differing Propensities to Consume Across Households," *Journal of Monetary Economics*, vol. 36, no. 2 (November 1995), pp. 301-327 for evidence that the wealthy have higher marginal propensities to save than low wealth households.

In: Federal Taxation
Editor: Jaclyn N. Prichard

ISBN: 978-1-61324-102-8

Chapter 6

CAPITAL GAINS TAXES: AN OVERVIEW*

Jane G. Gravelle

SUMMARY

Tax legislation in 1997 reduced capital gains taxes on several types of assets, imposing a 20% maximum tax rate on long-term gains, a rate temporarily reduced to 15% for 2003-2008, which was extended for two additional years in 2006. Legislation enacted in December 2010 extended the lower rates for an additional two years, thorough 2010.There is also an exclusion of $500,000 ($250,000 for single returns) for gains on home sales. The capital gains tax has been a tax cut target since the 1986 Tax Reform Act treated capital gains as ordinary income. An argument for lower capital gains taxes is reduction of the lock-in effect. Some also believe that lower capital gains taxes will cost little compared to the benefits they bring and that lower taxes induce additional economic growth, although the magnitude of these potential effects is in some dispute. Others criticize lower capital gains taxes as benefitting higher income individuals and express concerns about the budget effects, particularly in future years. Another criticism of lower rates is the possible role of a larger capital gains tax differential in encouraging tax sheltering activities and adding complexity to the tax law.

---

* This is an edited, reformatted and augmented version of Congressional Research Services publication 96-769, dated January 5, 2011.

WHAT ARE CAPITAL GAINS AND HOW ARE THEY TAXED?

Capital gain arises when an asset is sold and consists of the difference between the basis (normally the acquisition price) and the sales price. Corporate stock accounts for 20% to 80% of taxable gains, depending on stock market performance. Real estate is the remaining major source of capital gains, although gain also arises from other assets (e.g., timber sales and collectibles). The appreciation in value can be real or reflect inflation. Corporate stock appreciates both because the firm's assets increase with reinvested earnings and because general price levels are rising. Appreciation in the value of property may simply reflect inflation. For depreciable assets, some of the gain may reflect the possibility that the property was depreciated too quickly.

If the return to capital gains were to be effectively taxed at the statutory tax rate in the manner of other income, real gains would have to be taxed in the year they accrue. Current practice departs from this approach. Gains are not taxed until realized, benefitting from the deferral of taxes. (Taxes on interest income are due as the interest is accrued.) Gains on an asset held until death may be passed on to heirs with the tax forgiven; if the asset is then sold, the gain is sales price less market value at the time of death, a treatment referred to as a "step-up in basis."

Under current law, there is a maximum tax of 20% on capital gains held for a year (temporarily reduced to 15% for 2003-2012), although the ordinary income tax rates reach as high as 39.6% (temporarily reduced to 35%). Where ordinary tax rates are 15% or below, the capital gains tax is 10% (temporarily at 5% for 2003-2007 and 0% for 2008-2012). Assuming the temporary provisions expire, gain from assets held five years and acquired after 2000 will be subject to a maximum rate of 18%. For gains in the 15% bracket and below, an 8% rate will apply to any gain on assets held for five years and sold after 2000, with no required acquisition date. Gain arising from prior depreciation deductions is taxed at ordinary rates, but there is a 25% ceiling rate on the gain from attributable to prior straight-line depreciation on real property. Gain from collectibles is taxed at 28%.

Under law prior to 1997, several rules permitted avoidance or deferral of the tax on gain on owner-occupied housing, including a provision allowing deferral of gain until a subsequent house is sold (rollover treatment) and a provision allowing a one-time exclusion of $125,000 of gain for those 55 and over. These provisions were replaced with a general $500,000 exclusion ($250,000 for a single individual), which cost only slightly more in revenue.

In contrast to these provisions that benefit capital gains, capital gains are penalized because many of the gains that are subject to tax arise from inflation and therefore do not reflect real income.

A Brief History

Capital gains were taxed when the income tax (with rates up to 7%) was imposed in 1913. An alternative rate of 12.5% was allowed in 1921 (the regular top rate was 73%). Tax rates were cut several times during the 1920s. Capital gain exclusions based on holding period were enacted in 1924, and modified in 1938, to deal with bunching of gains in one year. In 1942 a 50% exclusion was adopted, with an alternative rate of 25%. Over time, the top rate on ordinary income varied, rising to 94% in the mid-1940s, then dropping to 70% after 1964. In 1969 a new minimum tax increased the gains tax for some; the 25% alternative tax was repealed.

In 1978 the minimum tax on capital gains was repealed and the exclusion increased to 60% with a maximum rate of 28% (0.4 times 0.7). The top rate on ordinary income was reduced to 50% in 1981, reducing the capital gains rate to 20% (0.4 times 0.5). The Tax Reform Act of 1986 reduced tax rates further, but, in order to maintain distributional neutrality, eliminated some tax preferences, including the exclusion for capital gains. This treatment brought the rate for high income individuals in line with the rate on ordinary income—28%.

In 1989, President Bush proposed a top rate of 15%, halving top rates. The Ways and Means Committee considered two proposals: Chairman Rostenkowski proposed to index capital gains, and Representatives Jenkins, Flippo, and Archer proposed a 30% capital gains exclusion through 1991 followed by inflation indexation. This latter measure was approved by the Committee, but was not enacted.

In 1990, the President proposed a 30% exclusion, setting the rate at 19.6% for high income individuals. The House also passed a 50% exclusion with a lifetime maximum ceiling and a $1,000 annual exclusion, but this provision was not enacted into law. When rates on high income individuals were set at 31%, however, the capital gains rate was capped at 28%.

In 1991, the President again proposed a 30% exclusion, but no action was taken. In 1992, the President proposed a 45% exclusion. The House adopted a proposal for indexation for inflation for newly acquired assets: the Senate passed a separate set of graduated rates on capital gains that tended to benefit more moderate income individuals. This latter provision was included in a bill (H.R. 4210) containing many other tax provisions that was vetoed by the President.

No changes were proposed by President Clinton or adopted in 1993 and 1994 with the exception of a narrowly targeted benefit for small business stock adopted in 1993. The value of the tax cap was increased, however, in 1993 when new brackets of 36% and 39.6% were added for ordinary income.

In 1994, the "Contract With America" proposed a 50% exclusion for capital gains, and indexing the basis for all subsequent inflation, while eliminating the 28% cap; this exclusion would be about a 40% reduction on average from current rates. The Ways and Means Committee reported out H.R. 1215 which restricted inflation indexing to newly acquired assets (individuals could "mark to market"—pay tax on the difference between fair market value and basis as if the property were sold to qualify for indexation), did not allow indexation to create losses and provided a flat 25% tax rate for corporations). The 1995 reconciliation bill (H.R. 2491) that was vetoed by the President, included these revisions but delayed the indexation provision until 2002. During the 1996 presidential election, Mr. Dole proposed a slightly larger capital gains cut, and both candidates supported elimination of capital gains taxes on virtually all gains from home sales.

In 1997, the President and Congress agreed to a tax cut as part of the reconciliation. The Administration tax cut proposal included the change in tax treatment of owner occupied housing. The House bill included a reduction in the 15% and 28% rates to 10% and 20%, about a 30% cut. Capital gains would also be indexed for assets acquired after 2000 and held for three years; markto-market would also be allowed. The Senate and the final bill did not include indexing. The capital gains issue was briefly revisited in 1998, when the holding period for long term gains was moved back from the 18 months set in 1997 to the one year period that has typically applied. The 1999 House bill would have cut the rates to 15% and 10%: the conference version cut rates to 18% and 8% and proposed indexing of future gains, but the bill was vetoed. Capital gains were discussed during the consideration of the economic stimulus bill at the end of 2002, but not included in any legislative proposal (and no proposal was adopted). The temporary provisions for lower rates of 15% for 2003-2008 for those in the higher brackets and to 5% in 2003-2007 and 0% in 2008 for taxpayers in the 15% bracket or lower were adopted in 2003. H.R. 4297, adopted in 2006, extended these lower rates for two more years. P.L. 111-312, enacted in 2010, extended the lower rates for an additional two years, through 2010.

REVENUE EFFECTS

Over the past several years, a debate has ensued regarding the revenue cost of cutting capital gains taxes. For example, when the President proposed a 30% exclusion in 1990, Treasury estimates showed a $12 billion gain in revenue over the first five years, while the Joint Committee on Taxation found a revenue loss of approximately equal size.

Although the estimates seemed quite different, they both incorporated significant expected increases in the amount of gains realized as a result of the tax cut. For example, the Treasury would have estimated a revenue loss of $80 billion over five years with no behavioral response, and the Joint Tax Committee a loss of $100 billion. (The gap between these static estimates arose from differences in projections of expected capital gains, a volatile series that is quite difficult to estimate.)

Empirical evidence on capital gains realizations does not clearly point to a specific response and revenue cost. Recent research suggests long-run responses may be more modest than those suggested by the economics literature during the 1990 debate, but the short-run response is still difficult to ascertain. (For a survey of this literature, see Jane G. Gravelle, *The Economic Effects of Taxing Capital Income*, Cambridge, MA: MIT Press, 1984, pp. 143-151; see also Leonard Burman, *The Labyrinth of Capital Gains Tax Policy*, Washington, DC: The Brookings Institution, 1999, for a discussion of this issue and many others.) A review of recent developments in this literature is in CRS Report R41364, *Capital Gains Tax Options: Behavioral Responses and Revenues*, by Jane G. Gravelle.

Any revenue feedback effect will be smaller the larger the tax reduction. When the tax reduction is large, although there will be a larger response, any induced revenues will be taxed at the new lower rates. Thus, a 50% exclusion will not have as large a feedback effect relative to the static estimate as a 30% exclusion. Moreover, allowing a prospective tax cut that depends on selling and acquiring a new asset to qualify (or marking to market) as is the case for the reduction from 20% to 18% for five-year property causes a gain in the short run as well.

Arguments have also been made that a capital gains tax cut will induce additional savings, also resulting in a feedback effect as taxes are imposed on new income. This effect is uncertain, as it is not clear that an increase in the rate of return will increase savings (savings can decrease if the income effect is more powerful than the substitution effect) and what the magnitude of the response might be. (See Congressional Budget Office Memorandum, *An Analysis of the Potential Macroeconomic Effects of the Economic Growth Act of 1998*). There is also a debate about the effect of the capital gains tax on growth through its effect on innovation. Regardless of these empirical uncertainties, any effect of savings on taxable income in the short run is likely to be quite small due to the slow rate of capital accumulation. (Net savings are typically only about 2% to 3% of the capital stock, so that even a 10% increase in the savings rate would result in only a 2/10 to 3/10 of a percent first-year increase in the capital stock.) A related argument is that the tax cut will increase asset values; such an effect is only temporary, however, and will, if it occurs, only shift revenues from the future to the present. (For a discussion of savings and asset valuations, see testimony of Jane G. Gravelle, Congressional Research Service, before the Senate Finance Committee, February 15, 1995, and the House Ways and Means Committee, March 19, 1997.)

IMPACT ON EFFECTIVE TAX BURDENS

The tax burden on an investment is influenced by both the tax rate and any benefits allowed or penalties imposed. One way to measure this tax burden is to calculate a marginal effective tax rate that captures in a single number all of the factors that affect tax burden. It is the percentage difference between the before- and after-tax return to investment, or the estimated statutory rate that would be applied to economic income to give the taxpayer the same burden as the combination of tax benefits and penalties.

The effective tax rate on capital gains can be either higher or lower than the statutory rate, depending on the inflation rate relative to the real appreciation rate and the holding period. Also, assets held until death are not subject to tax. For example, under prior law, assuming a 20% statutory tax rate, the gain on a growth stock (paying no dividends) with a real appreciation rate of 7% and an inflation rate of 3% would, if held for one year, seven years, 20 years, and until death, be subject respectively to tax rates of 27%, 22%, 14%, and 0%. The rate on 7- and 20-year assets would be 18%, for effective tax rates of 19% and 12%. (With no inflation and a 20% rate, the rates would be 19%, 16%, 12% and 0%; inflation penalizes assets held a shorter period more heavily than assets held for a longer period). Since less than half of gains that are accrued are realized, the effective tax rate is probably lower than the statutory tax rate. These benefits are larger for individuals who in the highest tax brackets (31%, 36%, and 39.6%) because the capital gains tax rate is capped at 20%. The rates would be lowered proportionally with a 15% tax rate.

ISSUES: EFFICIENCY, GROWTH, DISTRIBUTION, AND COMPLEXITY

One argument in favor of reducing the capital gains tax is the lock-in effect. If this effect is large, the tax introduces significant distortions in behavior with relatively little revenue gain. Another way to reduce lock-in is accrual taxation (i.e., tax gains on a current basis as accrued), but this approach is only feasible when assets can be easily valued (e.g., publicly traded corporate stock). Another way to reduce lock-in is to tax gains passed on at death. These solutions may face technical problems and taxation of gains at death has been unpopular.

For owner-occupied housing, although there were many ways to avoid the tax under current law, the rules may have resulted in individuals remaining in houses that are too large if economic circumstances have declined (for example, through job loss or retirement or from a preference for a smaller home, or if there is relocation to a lower-cost area.)

A case might be made for lower capital gains taxes on corporate stock because corporate equity capital is subject to heavy taxation. This heavy taxation encourages corporations to take on too much debt and directs too much capital to the noncorporate sector. On the other hand, lower capital gains taxes increase the relative penalty that applies to dividends and introduce tax distortions in the decisions of the firm to retain earnings. This latter effect, however, does not occur under the temporary tax cuts that benefit dividends as well as capital gains.

Arguments have also been made that lower gains taxes will increase economic growth and entrepreneurship. Although evidence on the effect of tax cuts on savings rates and, thus, economic growth is difficult to obtain, most evidence does not indicate a large response of savings to an increase in the rate of return. Indeed, not all studies find a positive response, because a higher rate of return may allow individuals to save less while reaching their desired goal. (See Gravelle, *The Economics of Taxing Capital Income*, MIT Press, pp. 24-28, for a survey.) A more effective route to increasing savings may be to take revenues that might otherwise finance a tax cut and reduce the debt.

Although arguments are made that lower gains taxes stimulate innovation and entrepreneurship, there is little evidence in history to connect periods of technical advance with lower taxes or even high rates of return. The extent to which entrepreneurs take tax considerations into account is unclear; however, there is some reason to doubt that capital gains taxes are important in obtaining large amounts of venture capital, in part because much of this capital is supplied by those not subject to the capital gains tax (i.e., pension funds, foreign investors).

(See CRS Report RL30040, *Capital Gains Taxes, Innovation and Growth*, by Jane G. Gravelle, for a further discussion of capital gains taxes and venture capital.) Moreover, there is no evidence that longer corporate stock holding periods lead to more investments in long-term assets, including R&D, a rationale for lowering rates for assets with longer holding periods. (Note that indexing, initially proposed, and then dropped, favors assets with shorter holding periods.)

A major complaint made by some about lower gains rates cut is that they primarily benefit very high income individuals. Capital gains are concentrated among higher income individuals because these individuals tend to own capital and because they are likely to own capital that generates capital gains. For example, the Joint Committee on Taxation indicated that for 2005, 88% of the benefit of lower rates to individuals with incomes over $200,000 and 95% would go to individuals with incomes over $100,000. Individuals with $200,000 of income account for about 3% of taxpayers and individuals with incomes over $100,000 account for less about 14%. The distributional effects of the capital gains relief for homes is somewhat less concentrated at the higher end (although lower income individuals are much less likely to own homes). The revisions may also enhance horizontal equity by treating taxpayer in different circumstances more evenly.

Critics of lower capital gains taxes cite the contribution of preferential capital gains treatment to tax sheltering activities and complexity. For example, individuals may borrow (while deducting interest in full) to make investments that are eligible for lower capital gains tax rates, thereby earning high rates of return. These effects are, however, constrained in some cases (i.e., a passive loss restriction limits the deductions allowed in real estate ventures). Capital gains differentials complicate the tax law, especially as applied to depreciable assets where capital gains treatment can create incentives for churning assets unless recapture provisions are adopted. Indexing capital gains for inflation is more complicated than a simple exclusion, since different basis adjustments must apply to different vintages of assets and proper indexing of gains on depreciable property is especially difficult. Thus, foregoing indexing probably kept the tax law simpler.

In: Federal Taxation
Editor: Jaclyn N. Prichard
ISBN: 978-1-61324-102-8

Chapter 7

INCREASING THE SOCIAL SECURITY PAYROLL TAX BASE: OPTIONS AND EFFECTS ON TAX BURDENS*

Thomas L. Hungerford

SUMMARY

According to the Social Security Trustees, assets in the two Social Security trust funds will be exhausted by 2037, and, thereafter, Social Security payroll tax revenues will cover about three-quarters of promised benefits. Over the past decade several proposals have been put forward which could help to close the Social Security program's long-term financing gap. One proposal would increase the Social Security payroll tax base so that 90% of covered earnings are taxable— the same proportion as in 1982. This policy would increase the payroll taxes paid by higher-earning workers and not affect workers earning less than the current Social Security maximum taxable limit, which is $106,800 in 2010.

Some analysts have proposed raising the Social Security payroll tax base and reducing the payroll tax rate. This policy would increase the taxes paid by higher-earning workers and reduce taxes paid by low- and middle-income workers. This policy proposal could raise revenue for the Social Security program or be revenue neutral.

---

* A version of this chapter was also published in *Social Security: Background, Issues and Proposals,* edited by Jacob T. Álvarez, published by Nova Science Publishers, Inc. It was submitted for appropriate modifications in an effort to encourage wider dissemination of research.

Although the legislated Social Security payroll tax rate is 12.4%, the average Social Security payroll tax is slightly progressive throughout the bottom 80% of the income distribution in that lower-income families pay a lower proportion of income in payroll taxes than higher-income families. At the higher-income levels—the top 20%—the payroll tax is regressive in that the proportion of income paid in payroll taxes falls as income rises. The richest 1% of American families pay a smaller proportion of their income in payroll taxes than the poorest 20% of families.

Three policy options, which raise the payroll tax base, are examined; two of the policies also provide tax relief to low- and middle-income workers. Each of the three policies reduces the regressivity of the payroll tax at the upper end of the income distribution. Currently, less than 10% of families contain a worker earning more than the maximum taxable limit. Consequently, over 90% of families would be unaffected by increasing the maximum taxable limit. And if this change were combined with a payroll tax rate reduction, over 90% of families would pay lower payroll taxes.

It has been argued that the revenue increases from raising the payroll tax base would be significantly less than expected because of indirect behavioral changes by workers. These predicted behavioral effects would reduce taxable earnings, the proportion of family income subject to payroll taxes, and tax revenue. But recent research raises doubts concerning this position and suggests these behavioral effects would likely be negligible.

This report will not be updated.

INTRODUCTION

The payroll tax for Social Security and Medicare is the largest federal tax many lower-income families pay. The Congressional Budget Office (CBO) estimates that the poorest 20% of U.S. households paid about 8.5% of their income on social insurance payroll taxes in 2006.[1] In contrast, these lower-income households paid negative income taxes because of the refundable earned income and child tax credits. Indeed, a justification for the earned income credit (EIC) is "to provide work incentives and relief from income and Social Security taxes to low-income families who might otherwise need large welfare payments."[2]

The tax rate under current law on covered earnings is 12.4% for Social Security and 2.9% for Medicare.[3] Half of the tax rate is paid by the employee and the other half by the employer; the self-employed are responsible for the entire amount.[4] The tax rate for Social Security applies only on covered earnings below the maximum taxable limit, which is $106,800 for 2010.[5] The Medicare tax rate applies to all covered earnings.

The Social Security Trustees project that the assets in the two Social Security trust funds will be exhausted in 2037, and after that, Social Security payroll tax revenue will cover about three-quarters of promised benefits.[6] To help close Social Security's long-term financing gap, some analysts have proposed increasing the Social Security tax base by raising the maximum taxable limit so that 90% of aggregate covered earnings are taxable (the percentage in 1982).[7] CBO estimates that the maximum taxable limit would have to increase to $186,000 in 2008, almost double the current limit, so that 90% of covered earnings are taxable. It is estimated that this policy could increase payroll tax revenues by $503.4 billion over the 2010-2019 period.[8] Since 1982, the ratio of taxable earnings to covered earnings has fallen from 90%, reaching 82.7% in 2007.

Although most analysts advocate raising the maximum taxable limit to increase revenues for the Social Security program, some would use the increased revenues for other purposes. For example, one analyst suggested reducing the payroll tax rate and keeping it revenue-neutral by raising the maximum taxable limit.[9] This change would provide payroll tax relief to low- and middle-income workers.

This report examines changes in the distribution of the tax burden of three policies involving raising the Social Security maximum taxable limit.

TAXABLE AND COVERED EARNINGS

The portion of Social Security-covered earnings subject to the payroll tax has fluctuated since its inception. Taxable earnings as a percentage of covered earnings was 92.4% in 1940 and dropped as low as 71.3% in 1965. The trend in this percentage since 1950 is displayed in Figure 1. Prior to 1972, the Social Security maximum taxable limit was updated periodically by Congress, which contributed to the dramatic and abrupt fluctuations in the 1950s and 1960s. After 1972, the maximum taxable limit was automatically updated as annual average earnings increased, which moderated the fluctuations somewhat. In response to Social Security funding problems, the 1977 amendments to the Social Security Act increased the Social Security tax base by raising the maximum taxable limit so that 90% of covered earnings were taxable by 1982. This change explains the increase in the proportion of covered earnings that are taxable from 84% in 1976 to 90% in 1982. After 1982, the maximum taxable limit was automatically updated as annual average earnings increased.

Although the maximum taxable limit is updated annually in response to increases in average wages, the proportion of covered earnings subject to the payroll tax is not constant—it has fallen since 1983. A primary reason is an increase in wage inequality. Wages have become more unequally distributed since the early 1980s, mostly due to wage gains at the top of the income distribution.[10] Consequently, a larger share of earnings of high-wage workers will be above the maximum taxable limit.

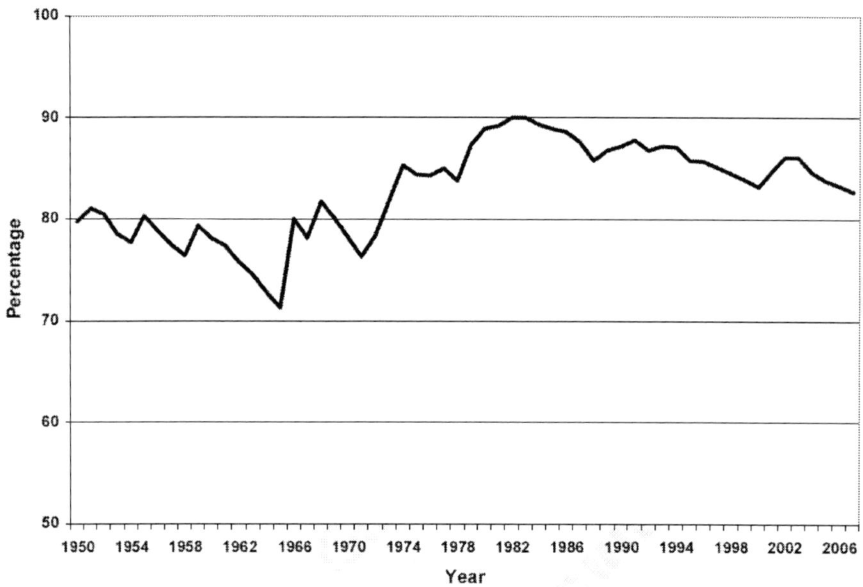

Source: Social Security Administration, 2007 Annual Statistical Supplement to the Social Security Bulletin, Table 4.B1.

Figure 1. Taxable Earnings as a Percentage of Social Security Covered Earnings, 1950-2007.

The Distribution of Tax Burdens

The distribution of tax burdens is simulated for three policy options, two of which have been proposed by various policy analysts. The base year for the simulation is 2008, the last year for which appropriate data is available.[11] The policy options compared in this report are:

- **Policy Option 1**. This policy would increase the maximum taxable limit to $186,000 (up from the 2008 limit of $102,000), which is the maximum taxable limit required so that 90% of covered earnings would have been subject to the payroll tax in 2007. The additional tax revenues are targeted to help close Social Security's projected long-term financing gap. Consequently, the payroll tax rate remains at 12.4%.
- **Policy Option 2**. This policy would also raise the maximum taxable limit to $186,000 but reduce the payroll tax rate to 11.4% so payroll tax revenues remain unchanged. In essence, the additional payroll tax revenues from increasing the maximum taxable limit are used to offset the reduction in the payroll tax rate.
- **Policy Option 3**. This policy option would raise the maximum taxable limit to $186,000. However, half of the additional revenue is targeted to reduce the projected long-term financing gap and the other half is used to offset a payroll tax rate reduction. The payroll tax rate is reduced to 11.9%.

Simulation results of the average Social Security tax rate for families with workers in different parts of the income distribution are reported in Table 1. The average tax rate is the total payroll tax (employee and employer shares) of each worker in the family and divided by total family income. Total family income includes wages, dividends, farm income, retirement income, royalties, and government cash transfers, among others. It does not include capital gains and in-kind government transfers such as food stamps and housing assistance. The average tax rate is reported for all families, each income quintile (20% of families), the richest 10% of families, the richest 5%, and the richest 1% of families.[12]

The first column of numbers in Table 1 shows the average tax rate under current law. The average tax rate for all families is 9.7%, which is less than the 12.4% statutory payroll tax rate on earnings. This occurs because only earnings are subject to the payroll tax while income from other sources is not. In addition, only the first $102,000 earned in 2008 was subject to the payroll tax while earnings above $102,000 were exempt.

Table 1. Average Social Security Payroll Tax Rates

		90% of Covered Payroll is Taxable		
	Current	Policy Option 1	Policy Option 2	Policy Option 3
All	9.66%	10.34%	9.50%	9.93%
Quintile 1	10.40	10.40	9.55	9.98
Quintile 2	10.55	10.55	9.69	10.13
Quintile 3	10.84	10.84	9.96	10.40
Quintile 4	10.97	11.03	10.14	10.59
Quintile 5	8.53	9.84	9.04	9.44
Top 10%	7.43	9.21	8.46	8.84
Top 5%	6.08	8.30	7.62	7.96
Top 1%	3.73	6.24	5.73	5.99

Source: Author's analysis of the March 2009 Current Population Survey.
Note: The sample includes only families that contain at least one worker.

The average tax rate, however, varies across the income distribution. Families in the poorest income quintile (that is, the poorest 20% of families) have an average tax rate of 10.4%. The average tax rate slightly increases in moving from the poorest quintile to the fourth quintile. Throughout the bottom 80% of the income distribution, the Social Security payroll tax is slightly progressive in that higher-income families pay a larger proportion of their income in payroll taxes than lower-income families.

The average tax rate for families in the richest income quintile, however, is 8.5%.[13] The rate falls in moving up through the upper part of the income distribution. The richest 10% of families pay a smaller share of income in payroll taxes than the poorest 20%, while the share of the richest 1% is about a third that of the poorest 20%. Above the 80th percentile, the payroll tax is a regressive tax in that the average tax rate falls as income rises.[14]

The second column of numbers shows the simulated average tax rates for policy option 1— raising the maximum taxable limit and maintaining the current legislated tax rate. For all families, the average tax rate rises by almost 0.7 percentage points (a 7% increase) to reach over 10%. This policy option, however, only affects workers whose earnings are above $102,000. Families in the bottom two income quintiles contain no workers earning more than $102,000, and about 0.1% of the families in the middle income quintile (quintile 3) contain such workers. Consequently, the average tax rates for the bottom three quintiles are largely unaffected by this policy option.

The average tax rate for the families in the top 40% of the income distribution, however, rises under policy option 1. The tax rate increases slightly for families in the fourth income quintile (from 10.97% to 11.03%) since only about 2% of these families contain a worker earning more than $102,000. The families in the top quintile, however, experience an 15% percent, or 1.3 percentage point, increase in their average tax rate. The average tax rate increases by 1.8 to 2.5 percentage points for families in the top 10% of the income distribution.

Policy option 2 raises the maximum taxable limit but reduces the tax rate so that total tax revenues remain unchanged. Since the policy is revenue neutral, the average tax rate for all families is the same as for current law (see the first row of Table 1). The average tax rate for most families, however, does change. The average rate falls for families in the bottom 80% of the income distribution (quintiles 1 to 4), and increases for families at the top. In general, workers earning less than $111,045 will pay less in payroll taxes than they do under current law; workers earning more than this will pay more in payroll taxes.

The final option, policy option 3, is a blend of the first two policy options. Half of the increased revenue from raising the maximum taxable limit is used for financing the Social Security program and the other half offsets a payroll tax rate reduction. As was the case with policy option 2, this policy option reduces the average tax rates for families in the bottom 80% of the income distribution and increases it for families in the top income quintile. For the richest 1% of families, this option raises the average tax rate by 2.3 percentage points, a 61% increase. The poorest 20% see their average tax rate fall by 0.4 percentage points, or by about 4%.

Table 2 provides an alternate view of the effects of the three policy options by reporting the simulated average dollar change in Social Security payroll taxes paid by families in different parts of the income distribution. The reported dollar amounts include the change in both the employee's and employer's portion of the payroll tax. It is important to keep in mind that a family may contain more than one worker.

The dollar changes are consistent with the changes in the average tax rates reported in Table 1. The first policy option increases the payroll tax for the average family by $488. This policy option does not affect families in the bottom two income quintiles and increases the tax payments for families in the middle quintile by only $1, on average. The average family in the richest income quintile would pay $1,948 more in taxes, and the richest 1% of families would pay, on average, $10,877 more in payroll taxes under this policy.

Table 2. Average Change in Annual Social Security Payroll Taxes

	Policy Option 1	Policy Option 2	Policy Option 3
All	$488	$0	$190
Quintile 1	$0	-$117	-$58
Quintile 2	$0	-$263	-$130
Quintile 3	$1	-$430	-$212
Quintile 4	$49	-$607	-$276
Quintile 5	$1,948	$754	$1,357
Top 10%	$3,460	$1,999	$2,737
Top 5%	$5,622	$3,908	$4,773
Top 1%	$10,877	$8,674	$9,786

Source: Author's analysis of the March 2009 Current Population Survey.
Note: The sample includes only families that contain at least one worker.

The second policy option is revenue neutral; consequently, the average tax change is zero. Families in the bottom four income quintiles would pay between $117 and $607 less in taxes, on average. Families in the top quintile would pay higher taxes (about $754, on average) and the richest 1% of families would pay $8,674 more.

The impact of policy option 3 on payroll tax payments follows the same patterns as policy option 2, but the amounts are larger. On average, families will pay $190 more in payroll taxes under this policy. However, families in the bottom 80% of the income distribution will pay lower taxes, on average. High-income families (the top quintile) pay $1,357 more in taxes, while the richest 1% pay about $9,800 more in payroll taxes.

BEHAVIORAL EFFECTS OF TAX CHANGES

It has been argued that the revenue increases from raising the payroll tax base would be significantly less than expected because of indirect behavioral changes by workers. Based on this interpretation, workers may respond to having more earnings subject to the payroll tax, which in effect is a reduction in earnings, by reducing their work effort (a labor supply effect) or shifting their income to forms that are not subject to the payroll tax (a taxable income effect). These behavioral effects would thus reduce taxable earnings, the proportion of family income subject to payroll taxes, and tax revenue.[15] As discussed below, however, recent research raises doubts concerning this position and suggests these behavioral effects would likely be negligible.

Relatively few families would be negatively affected by the three policy options examined. Of the families with at least one worker, about 10% contain a worker earning more than the maximum taxable limit (see Table 3). Families in the bottom two income quintiles contain no workers earning more than the maximum taxable limit ($102,000 in 2008). And few families in the next two quintiles contain high-earning workers—0.1% of the families in the middle quintile and about 2% of the fourth quintile. About 30% of the families in the richest income quintile contain workers earning more than the maximum taxable limit. The percentage is significantly higher for the richest 10% of families. Consequently, most of the 6% of families with high-earning workers are at the top of the income distribution—71% are in the richest 10% of U.S. families.

For the few families with high-earning workers, changing the payroll tax rate can affect labor supply in two possible ways. The first is the direct effect in which tax changes affect the wage received by the worker. Reducing wages could lead to a reduction in work effort (that is, labor supply). The empirical evidence indicates that men's labor supply is relatively inelastic (that is, changes in the wage have little effect on labor supply) with estimated elasticities close to zero.[16] In the past, women's labor force behavior differed significantly from that of men. This was especially true for married women. But recent research indicates a convergence in the labor force behavior of the sexes. A recent study suggests that over the past two decades, women's labor supply elasticities have fallen and converged with that of men.[17] One study, specifically examining the effect of the payroll tax on women's labor supply, concludes there is a work disincentive effect for women over 50.[18] Since about 3.5% of women over 50 earn more than the maximum taxable limit, few would potentially be affected by the three policy options analyzed. Furthermore, this study is based on labor force data from the 1970s—a time when women's labor supply was more responsive to wage changes.

Table 3. High-Earning Workers and Taxable Earnings by Quintile, 2008

	Percentage of Families with at Least One Worker Earning More than Maximum Taxable Limit	Taxable Earnings as a Percentage of Total Family Income
All	6.4%	77.9%
Quintile 1	0.0	83.8
Quintile 2	0.0	85.1
Quintile 3	0.1	87.4
Quintile 4	2.1	88.4
Quintile 5	29.9	68.8
Top 10%	49.1	60.0
Top 5%	72.2	49.0
Top 1%	98.5	30.1

Source: Author's analysis of the March 2009 Current Population Survey.
Note: The sample includes only families that contain at least one worker.

The second effect is an indirect effect in which a change in the wage of one spouse affects the labor supply of the other spouse. Empirical studies, however, suggest married men are largely unresponsive to changes in their wives' wages with estimated elasticities close to zero.[19] While women's labor supply, however, is thought to be responsive to changes in their husband's wage, recent research suggests women's responsiveness has declined over the past two decades.[20]

The cited studies suggest that raising the maximum taxable limit will have little effect on workers' labor supply. Relatively few workers earn enough to be affected by such a policy change (about 7% of all workers earn more than the maximum taxable limit). Additionally, men's labor supply appears largely unaffected by changes in their own wage and their spouse's wage. And women's labor supply behavior has increasingly become like that of men, and consequently they too appear largely unaffected by changes in their own wage and their spouse's wage.

While work effort or labor supply may not be affected by changes in the payroll tax, earnings subject to the payroll tax may be affected. In the aggregate, about three-quarters of U.S. families' income comes from taxable earnings (see the last column of Table 3). Of the rest, most comes from earnings above the maximum taxable limit, retirement income (Social Security and pension income), and investment returns (interest, dividends, and rental income). The proportion of family income from taxable earnings is over 80% for the bottom 80% of the income distribution. While the richest 20% of families derive about 69% of their income from taxable earnings. This proportion falls to under 50% for the richest 5% of families, and to about 30% for the richest 1%. Consequently, there may be some opportunities for workers with earnings more than the maximum taxable limit to shift their earnings to a nontaxable form of compensation.

The economics research before 2000 generally suggests taxable income is responsive to changes in marginal tax rates.[21] As marginal tax rates rise, the pre-2000 studies indicate taxpayers reduced their taxable income through tax avoidance strategies or tax evasion. They can do this by increasing deductions to reduce taxable income or by taking compensation in forms that are untaxed (such as stock options, which are untaxed until exercised) or subject to lower tax rates. Arecent study, however, concludes that methodological problems lead to the estimated elasticities likely being overstated.[22]

More recent research suggests that the earlier results may have been due to the behavior of a few taxpayers in the extreme upper part of the income distribution.[23] Several recent studies estimate that taxable income is much less responsive to changes in tax rates and suggest that relatively large increases in tax rates could lead to relatively small decreases in taxable income.[24] In addition, one study found that tax rate changes have no effect on wages, one component of taxable income.[25] Raising the maximum taxable limit would increase the marginal tax rate on wages, but this recent empirical research suggests that workers' wage earnings would be largely unaffected.[26] This research also suggests that reducing the payroll tax rate (as in policy options 2 and 3) would not affect workers' behavior.

End Notes

[1] CBO, *Historical Effective Federal Tax Rates: 1979 to 2006*, April 2009. Social insurance payroll taxes include Social Security and Medicare payroll plus Unemployment Insurance payroll taxes.

[2] U.S. Congress, Joint Committee on Taxation, *General Explanation of the Revenue Act of 1978*, joint committee print, 96th Cong., 1st sess., Mar. 12, 1979 (Washington: GPO, 1979), p. 51.

[3] Covered earnings are earnings from employment covered by the Social Security and Medicare programs. Most workers in the United States are covered by the Social Security and Medicare programs. Some federal, state, and local workers, however, are not covered by these programs. The Health Care and Education Reconciliation Act of 2010 (P.L. 111-152) increased the Medicare payroll by 0.9 percentage points for high income taxpayers (to 3.8%).

[4] Most economists agree that workers ultimately bear the full burden of the payroll tax. Employers typically pass on their share of the payroll tax to employees through paying lower wages. See CBO, *Effective Federal Tax Rates, 1979- 1997*, October 2001.

[5] The maximum taxable limit is adjusted annually to keep pace with changes in average earnings. Covered earnings below the maximum taxable limit are referred to as taxable earnings.

[6] This projection is based on the Trustees' intermediate cost assumptions. Under the low cost assumptions, Social Security does not face long-term financial problems, and under the high cost assumptions, the Social Security trust funds will be depleted in 2031. See The Board of Trustees, *The 2009 Annual Report of the Board of Trustees of the Federal Old-Age and Survivors Insurance and Federal Disability Insurance Trust Funds*, May 12, 2009 (Washington: GPO, 2009).

[7] Provisions in the 1977 amendments to the Social Security Act were designed to increase the percentage of covered earnings subject to the payroll tax to 90% by 1982.

[8] CBO, *Budget Options*, volume 2, August 2009, p. 234.

[9] Dalton Conley, "Turning the Tax Tables to Help the Poor," *New York Times*, Nov. 15, 2004, p. A21.

[10] Robert G. Valletta, *Computer Use and the U.S. Wage Distribution, 1984-2003*, Federal Reserve Bank of San Francisco Working Paper 2006-34, October 2006.

[11] The data source for the simulations is the Annual Social and Economic Supplement of the March 2009 Current Population Survey (CPS). For this survey, the Census Bureau collects survey information for over 200,000 people living in almost 100,000 households. The survey is representative of the civilian noninstitutionalized population in the United States. The March supplement includes detailed information on family and individual income for the previous year.

[12] Families are assigned to income quintiles based on equivalence-adjusted total family income (total family income divided by an equivalence scale). The equivalence scale is the one proposed by the National Research Council. See Constance F. Citro and Robert T. Michael, eds., *Measuring Poverty: A New Approach* (Washington, DC: National Academy Press, 1995).

[13] The average tax rate for high-income families may be artificially high because income components are top-coded (that is, cut-off at a particular amount) in the CPS by the Census Bureau to prevent identification of high-income individuals.

[14] The results are broadly consistent with an analysis by CBO. Any differences are due to differences in the unit of analysis (family versus household), income definition and data source. See CBO, *Historical Effective Federal Tax Rates: 1979 to 2006*, April 2009.

[15] D. Mark Wilson, *Removing Social Security's Tax Cap on Wages Would Do More Harm Than Good*, Heritage Foundation, Center for Data Analysis Report #01-07, Oct. 17, 2001.

[16] Mark R. Killingsworth, *Labor Supply* (New York: Cambridge University Press, 1983), and Richard Blundell and Thomas MaCurdy, "Labor Supply: A Review of Alternative Approaches," in Orley Ashenfelter and David Card, eds., *Handbook of Labor Economics* (Amsterdam: Elsevier, 1999), pp. 1559-1695.

[17] Francine D. Blau and Lawrence M. Kahn, "Changes in the Labor Supply Behavior of Married Women: 1980-2000," *Journal of Labor Economics*, vol. 25, no. 3 (July 2007), pp. 393-438.

[18] Therese A. McCarty, "The Effect of Social Security on Married Women's Labor Force Participation," *National Tax Journal*, vol. 43, no. 1 (March 1990), pp. 95-110.

[19] Paul J. Devereux, "Changes in Relative Wages and Family Labor Supply," *Journal of Human Resources*, vol. 39 (Summer 2004), pp. 696-722, and Francine D. Blau and Lawrence M. Kahn, *Changes in the Labor Supply Behavior of Married Women: 1980-2000*, National Bureau of Economic Research, Working Paper no. 11230, March 2005.

[20] Francine D. Blau and Lawrence M. Kahn, *Changes in the Labor Supply Behavior of Married Women: 1980-2000*, National Bureau of Economic Research, Working Paper no. 11230, March 2005.

[21] Martin Feldstein, "The Effect of Marginal Tax Rates on Taxable Income: A Panel Study of the 1986 Tax Reform Act," *Journal of Political Economy*, vol. 103, no. 3 (1995), pp. 551-572; and Gerald Auten and Robert Carroll, "The Effect of Income Taxes on Household Behavior," *Review of Economics and Statistics*, vol. 81, no. 3 (1999), pp. 681-693.

[22] CRS Report RL33672, *Revenue Feedback from the 2001-2004 Tax Cuts*, by Jane G. Gravelle.

[23] Robert A. Moffitt and Mark O. Wilhelm, "Taxation and the Labor Supply Decisions of the Affluent," in Joel B. Slemrod, ed., *Does Atlas Shrug? The Economic Consequences of Taxing the Rich* (Cambridge, MA: Harvard University Press, 2002).

[24] Jon Gruber and Emmanuel Saez, "The Elasticity of Taxable Income: Evidence and Implications," *Journal of Public Economics*, vol. 84 (2002), pp. 1-32; and Emmanuel Saez, "The Effect of Marginal Tax Rates on Income: A Panel Study of 'Bracket Creep,'" *Journal of Public Economics*, vol. 87 (2003), pp. 1231-1258.

[25] Emmanuel Saez, "The Effect of Marginal Tax Rates on Income: A Panel Study of 'Bracket Creep,'" *Journal of Public Economics*, vol. 87 (2003), pp. 1231-1258.

[26] Workers with earnings above the higher maximum taxable limit of $213,900 would not face an increase in the marginal tax rate after the change—their marginal tax rate would remain at zero.

In: Federal Taxation
Editor: Jaclyn N. Prichard

ISBN: 978-1-61324-102-8

Chapter 8

THE ROLE OF FEDERAL GASOLINE EXCISE TAXES IN PUBLIC POLICY*

Robert Pirog

SUMMARY

American drivers, compared to those in other industrialized nations in Europe, pay relatively low federal, state, and local gasoline and diesel excise taxes. The federal taxes are used specifically to fund annual highway construction, maintenance, and mass transit. Over the years, proposals have come forth to raise the federal tax as a way to address long-standing national policy concerns, including U.S. dependence on imported oil and various environmental problems related to large volumes of gasoline consumption.

Policy attention on the role of the gasoline tax has also increased recently due to three major developments. First, the 2008 oil and gasoline price run-up and subsequent economic downturn have led to a decline in gasoline tax revenues available for needed highway construction and maintenance. Second, the possibility of enacting some form of binding climate change legislation in the next several years will eventually mean an increase in the relative price of fossil fuels, including oil and gasoline. Third, the volatility of gasoline prices has affected investment planning (e.g. for alternative fuels) and arguably contributed to the troubles facing domestic automobile manufacturers. In the above context, this report outlines some of the macroeconomic and microeconomic pros and cons of using the federal

* This is an edited, reformatted and augmented version of Congressional Research Services publication R40808, dated April 15, 2010.

gasoline excise tax for policy purposes in addition to the funding of highway infrastructure.

Whether an increase in the gasoline tax was fixed or variable, advocates argue that increasing the relative price of gasoline would promote beneficial short- and long-term changes in how we use this form of energy. A higher relative price would encourage consumers and manufacturers to move toward more fuel-efficient vehicles, or to switch to alternative fuels, thus reducing oil consumption and imports, reducing air pollution, and possibly encouraging greater use of mass transit. Advocates further argue that such taxes could be recycled back into the economy through changes in the tax structure and/or increased investment in renewable or alternative fuels, among other options.

Opponents of gasoline tax increases point to the effects on consumer and business spending, which affect the short- and long-term performance of the overall U.S. economy, especially in a time of needed economic recovery. Additionally, opponents point out that the gasoline tax has a regressive impact and affects rural areas disproportionately. Opponents also argue that such tax revenues could be better spent if left in the private sector.

Gasoline price increases due to market forces, or earlier tax increases, of course, have been part of the economic environment for almost four decades. Since the mid-1970s, there have been significant spikes in gasoline prices due to world oil market turmoil attributed to political conflict and war in the Middle East and to financial market speculation. Depending on the specified purpose of a new gasoline tax increase, it could be modest, or more significant. Because the demand for gasoline is quite price insensitive (inelastic), significant revenues could be generated with little change in real consumption, even with a relatively low tax increase. A more substantial tax increase would likely be needed to change consumer preferences and business investment decisions. Any debate on modifying the gasoline excise tax will likely revolve around these tensions.

INTRODUCTION

Gasoline taxes affect both the national economy and the decisions of individual consumers. If set at a sufficiently high level, they can reduce consumption to levels that reflect the adverse effects of gasoline use, including environmental damage and security costs. However, they can also slow the level of macroeconomic activity, despite contributing to lower trade deficits by reducing the need for imported oil. If, as in the United States, federal gasoline tax revenues are directly tied to financing highway construction and maintenance, they can also create jobs and improve the national infrastructure. If the gasoline tax is designed in such a way that the price of gasoline is stabilized, more informed decisions concerning the purchase of fuel-efficient vehicles and the funding of mass transit might also be made.

It is widely believed that the federal gasoline tax is unpopular with consumers and that increasing the tax will likely generate opposition. However, the federal tax on gasoline is relatively low, only 6.5% of the average price per gallon in April 2010, and less than 5% of the average price in the summer of 2008, the most recent peak in gasoline prices. The tax raises revenue for highway construction and maintenance, which is directly related to automobile and gasoline use, suggesting that the tax is in the nature of a user charge. Many attempts to increase the tax since the early 1970s, especially those tied to energy policy initiatives, have been defeated; however, over that period the tax increased in several steps from 4 cents per gallon to the current rate of 18.4 cents per gallon.

Although the federal gasoline tax is collected at the refinery, it is fully passed on to consumers, along with state and local taxes, and is included in the pump price.[1]

This report examines the effects of the federal excise tax on gasoline and analyzes the positive and negative effects of the tax. The report also evaluates the incentive structure that a higher gasoline tax would likely create, and examines a revised version of the tax, a variable gasoline tax.

BACKGROUND

Excise taxes are, in effect, sales taxes levied on specific goods. The tax may be set either as a percent of the value of the good, an ad valorem tax, or as a set dollar value per unit of the good, a unit tax. Excise taxes have been used to provide general, or dedicated, revenue and deficit reduction, but in some cases, for example liquor and cigarettes, there is a presumption that discouraging consumption in addition to raising revenues is a motivating factor in enacting the tax.

The first excise tax on motor fuels in the United States was enacted by Oregon in 1919. Within 13 years, every state and the District of Columbia had enacted similar taxes ranging from 2 to 7 cents per gallon. The federal government levied its first excise tax on gasoline in 1932 at the rate of 1 cent per gallon as a general revenue tax. The federal excise tax became permanent in 1941 under Section 521 (a)(20) of the Revenue Act of 1941.[2]

Gasoline for use on highways is currently taxed by the federal government at 18.4 cents per gallon. Of this 18.4-cents-per-gallon tax, 18.3 cents per gallon is earmarked for the Highway Trust Fund, and 0.1 cents per gallon is allocated to the

Leaking Underground Storage Tank (LUST) Trust Fund. The total excise tax on gasoline, at the retail level, is in the range of approximately 40 cents to over 50 cents per gallon, depending on the specific state and local taxes that are added to the federal tax. Federal, as well as most state and local levies, are unit taxes, and as such, do not vary with the price of gasoline, as a tax based on ad valorem rates would.

While opposition to the federal gasoline tax has existed since its inception, the direct tie to the Highway Trust Fund, the expansion of the interstate highway system, and highway projects to ease road congestion, has led to the view that the tax might be a proxy for a user charge, or price, to consumers who directly benefit from services provided through the tax, easing opposition to some extent.

After the oil embargo of 1973-1974, interest in the use of the gasoline tax as a policy instrument expanded to areas beyond highway financing. The Nixon Administration considered using a gasoline tax increase as a way of reducing inflationary pressures in the economy. During the Ford Administration, Representative Al Ullman introduced legislation to increase gasoline taxes to fund alternative energy sources by allocating revenues to a proposed trust fund. The Carter Administration embraced the idea of escalating gasoline taxes as a part of an energy program in 1977 designed to reduce oil consumption and increase U.S. energy security. After the fall of the Shah of Iran in 1979 and the Iran-Iraq war that began in 1980, gasoline prices increased to then-record levels and interest in gasoline taxes as a way to reduce foreign oil dependence was suggested by independent presidential candidate John Anderson. The Carter Administration proposed an oil import fee in March 1980 that was intended to approximate the effect of a gasoline tax. None of these proposals were successfully passed into law by Congress.[3]

In 1982, the Reagan Administration proposed an increase in the federal gasoline tax for the purpose of improving and repairing the nation's highways, based on the user-fee nature of the tax. Within the Administration, the fact that the tax was likely to create jobs was also considered as a reason for the tax increase, although President Reagan did not support government-funded jobs programs, or tax increases. The Reagan gasoline tax increase passed in both the House and the Senate and was signed into law on January 5, 1983. It raised the federal tax from 4 cents per gallon to 9 cents per gallon.

A further increase in the gasoline tax was included in the Omnibus Budget Reconciliation Act of 1990, but the rationale for the tax increase was deficit reduction. President George H. W. Bush initially opposed the tax increase, but then reversed himself and supported it, and signed the Omnibus Budget

Reconciliation Act of 1990 into law on November 5, 1990, raising the federal gasoline tax to 14.1 cents per gallon.

President Bill Clinton initially supported a broad-based energy tax rather than a gasoline tax. The Administration decided to propose a tax on the energy content of fuels, a British Thermal Unit (B.T.U.) tax. This tax proposal failed to gain support in Congress, and, as an alternative, an increase in the gasoline tax to 18.4 cents per gallon was passed by Congress and signed by President Clinton, and took effect in December 1993. The revenue from the tax increase, 4.3 cents per gallon, was restricted to be allocated to deficit reduction. The latter part of the 1990s was characterized by declining federal deficits as tax revenues rose, as well as low gasoline prices, taking increases in the gasoline tax off the policy agenda.[4]

President George W. Bush's Administration did not propose any increase in the gasoline tax. However, there were calls for a temporary reduction in the tax to help American drivers who paid record high prices for gasoline in the summer of 2008.[5]

The Obama Administration has opposed an increase in the gasoline tax during the recession. However, it has advocated a number of policy objectives—greenhouse gas reduction, energy security, economic stimulus, more fuel efficiency, and moving toward alternative energy sources—that have been discussed in the past as justifications for gasoline tax increases.

ECONOMIC EFFECTS

The purpose of a tax is to fund government through a transfer of resources from the taxpayer to the government. As a result, every tax leaves the taxpayers with less purchasing power than they had before the tax was levied. However, the government may use the resources acquired through the tax revenue to finance the provision of public goods and services for the benefit of the taxpayers.[6] Because it is unlikely that every taxpayer can agree about the proper mix and level of every public good and service, as well as every choice and level of tax instrument, taxes are unlikely to be voluntary, and the government must use the force of law to levy and collect taxes.

In addition, taxes can have a wide variety of economic effects, from altering consumer decisions concerning mix of goods to purchase, to national macroeconomic issues of economic growth, employment, and inflation.

Changing Demand-Supply Relationships

The legal, or statutory, incidence of an excise tax on gasoline is on the refiner; however, the tax is typically passed on to the consumer, and is paid at the pump along with state and local taxes, leaving the economic incidence of the tax with the consumer. This result is in accord with economic theory that suggests that if the demand for the product is totally inelastic the firm will pass the tax on to consumers who will pay the tax, independent of the nature of supply. Although the demand for gasoline is not totally inelastic in the short run, its elasticity is very low, approximating total inelasticity. Analytic studies suggest that the elasticity of gasoline demand over a wide range of price variation is low, and perhaps near zero in the short run.[7] In the case of gasoline taxes, the supply side of the market is likely to support the demand side result because of the wide range of essentially constant cost output levels of gasoline from modern refineries.

When a tax alters consumers' or producers' economic decisions, the tax is said to have an excess burden, a burden beyond that of the tax revenue paid to the government. If an excise tax is levied on a good whose marginal social cost is greater than its marginal private cost, the excess burden, which shifts consumer's choices away from the taxed good, may be part of the design of the tax.[8]

In the case of gasoline, if it is hypothesized that gasoline use generates social costs—for example, national security and/or environmental issues—that raise its total cost above the private costs, then in an untaxed environment, it could be said that gasoline is being over-consumed. If one denies the linkage between social costs and gasoline consumption, then a free market-generated consumption level consistent with the price equalized with marginal private cost is appropriate on economic efficiency grounds. In the real-world market for gasoline, it is unclear whether the market result is efficient or not, because a variety of market imperfections related to actual or potential market power exist, making it difficult to determine whether actual consumption is greater, or lower, than the consumption level of the free market. These market power factors include a market dominated by a few large firms, the presence of the Organization of the Petroleum Exporting Countries (OPEC), and national oil companies exerting political influence on the world price of oil.

Even if it is accepted that gasoline consumption is associated with the generation of social costs, the level of the tax on a per-gallon basis must be determined. To encourage the use of alternative fuels, or to reduce petroleum imports and carbon emissions, the tax must be set high enough to cause consumers to decide that it is in their economic interest to substitute other energy sources, or to conserve. If the price elasticity of demand for gasoline is low, this implies that a relatively large tax will be necessary to result in a significant reduction in consumption.

An increase in the federal excise tax on gasoline would be a drain on consumer purchasing power, and could result in a slow-down in macroeconomic activity. However, part, or all, of the tax revenue raised could be returned to consumers through reductions in other taxes. A total return of tax revenue would not be appropriate if the purpose of the tax increase was to fund the Highway Trust Fund. If the purpose is to reduce the consumption of gasoline, then a return of tax revenue through reductions in other taxes is more reasonable.

Reducing Gasoline Price Volatility

Two key factors in explaining gasoline demand in the United States are price and consumer income. Economists have empirically estimated that in the short run, the sensitivity of the quantity demand of oil, and therefore, gasoline quantities, to price variations is low.[9] Low price elasticity of demand, a percentage quantity variation less than the percentage price variation, suggests that the good is viewed by consumers as a necessity, one that must be purchased with little quantity variation, even in the face of higher prices. Additionally, commodities with low price elasticity of demand tend to be subject to substantial price volatility when quantities available on the market vary.

Income elasticity measures how responsive consumer demand for a good is to changes in consumer income levels. Income and price elasticity can interact. For example, even if the price of a commodity increases, implying that the quantity demanded should fall in the proportion suggested by the price elasticity measure, the predicted demand reduction might not be observed in consumption data if income increases sufficiently, making any given expenditure on the good a smaller percentage of available income.

These concepts of price and income elasticity are likely to have important effects on the structure and level of an effective gasoline tax. Effective, in relation to a gasoline tax, can be defined in a variety of ways. One possible way to define effective with respect to a tax is its efficacy in providing government revenues, and/or reducing the consumption of gasoline, in a predictable manner that provides consistent incentives to consumers to make appropriate economic choices, in accordance with national economic goals.

U.S. gasoline consumption rose by 9.6% from 2000 to 2007 even as the nominal price of gasoline almost doubled.[10] Income growth, as well as a variety of other factors, contributed to the increasing demand, even as prices rose. Demand for gasoline began to decline in the fourth quarter of 2007, coincident with the onset of the current recession. The rise, and then peaking, of gasoline prices at over $4 per gallon in 2008 also contributed to the declining demand that resulted in the reduced demand that continued in 2009.[11]

The behavior of gasoline demand over the period from 2000 to 2009 has implications for the design of a gasoline tax. The current federal tax on gasoline is a fixed 18.4 cents per gallon. In addition, states and localities generally add their own taxes on gasoline. The current tax does not appear to be functioning as an effective tax, by the definition set out above; it is not raising adequate revenues, reducing consumption, or providing consistent incentives. On the revenue side, the federal gasoline tax, along with the corresponding tax on diesel fuel (24.4 cents per gallon) provided over $30 billion in revenue to the Highway Trust Fund in FY2008; however, the Highway Trust Fund, the financing of which depends on fuel excise taxes for about 90% of its funding, is relatively unstable financially.[12] In addition, because the existing federal tax is relatively small, compared to the price of gasoline, and is a declining portion of consumer income, as incomes rise, it likely is not having as large an effect in reducing consumption as it might have had when it was instituted. Reducing gasoline consumption is a goal consistent with achieving less dependence on imported crude oil, and reducing greenhouse gas emissions.

Since the federal gasoline tax is a fixed amount per gallon, and small relative to the price of gasoline, it does little to provide incentives to consumers to consider fuel-efficient vehicles. When the price of gasoline rises, and attains high levels, consumer interest in fuel efficiency increases, but when gasoline prices fall, their interest wanes. Volatile gasoline prices cause this cycle to repeat itself. As a result, consumers tend to buy the "wrong type" of vehicle for the next gasoline price cycle.

On the production side, consumers' shifting automobile preferences have contributed to the instability in the auto industry. The high gasoline prices in 2008 shifted consumer demand away from sport utility vehicles and light trucks, profit centers for the U.S. auto manufacturers, and helped push General Motors and Chrysler to bankruptcy. As these firms emerge from bankruptcy, their plans to introduce fuel-efficient cars that they can sell profitably could be problematic if gasoline were to fall below $2 per gallon and remain there for a significant time.

One way to overcome these uncertainties, if it is the policy to discourage gasoline consumption in order to lessen dependence on imported oil and to reduce greenhouse gas emissions, is through a variable gasoline tax. A variable gasoline tax would target a specific price of gasoline (including tax) that was thought by policy makers to achieve desirable levels of gasoline consumption and/or revenue production. When the price of oil rises, increasing the cost of gasoline above the target price, the tax would remain constant, and consumption would fall in response to market forces. Alternatively, if gasoline prices fell, the tax would automatically rise to keep the price including tax at the target price level. In this way, the tax would provide a more constant incentive to consumers to purchase fuel-efficient vehicles, drive less, and encourage interest in alternative fuel vehicles.

Economists identify two factors in consumer purchases, the substitution effect and the income effect. A tax raises the relative price of gasoline relative to other goods, causing consumers to respond with a decision to buy less of the good; this is called the substitution effect. Taxes also make the taxed goods more expensive, reducing consumers' general purchasing power; this is called the income effect. Even if the income effect is reversed through a tax rebate program, the substitution effect will still encourage lower consumption of the taxed commodity. In this way, the tax could have a minimal effect on purchasing power if consumers chose to follow market economic incentives and minimize consumption of the taxed good. If they chose to attempt to continue to consume at pre-tax levels, purchasing power would be reduced, but that would be the free choice of the consumer.

The variable gasoline tax, set at a sufficiently high level to affect consumer decisions, could be expected to stimulate the demand for smaller, more fuel-efficient automobiles, spur the development of cars that use alternative energy sources, reduce U.S. oil imports and dependence on supplies from unstable parts of the world, reduce greenhouse gas emissions, and reduce the costs of maintaining the highway and road system, as well as likely reduce the number of accidents and fatalities.

Table 1. Comparative Gasoline Prices and Taxes, 2008 (dollars per gallon)

	United States	**United Kingdom**	**Germany**	**France**
Retail Price	3.24	7.53	7.72	7.53
Price, Ex Tax	2.84	2.88	2.86	2.96
Tax	0.41	4.65	4.86	4.57

Source: Energy Information Administration, available at http://www.eia.doe.gov/emeu/international/gas1.html. Notes: In some cases, data is not consistent with respect to fuel grade.

While U.S consumers have enjoyed low taxes on gasoline for some time, taxes in other industrialized nations are higher. As shown in Table 1, in 2008 gasoline prices ex tax were within a 5% spread, but the price of gasoline including taxes was almost 2.5 times higher in the European nations. High gasoline taxes in Europe have provided incentives for consumers to buy smaller cars, drive less, and switch to diesel fuel, which offers better fuel economy than comparable gasoline-fueled automobiles.

As gasoline prices have fallen during the first half of 2009, retail prices have declined in all the countries cited in Table 1. However, the European prices range from $4.88 per gallon in the United Kingdom to $5.74 per gallon in Germany and $5.54 per gallon in France, while the U.S. price fell to $1.91 per gallon.

Although the gasoline taxes in the countries identified in Table 1 are not variable, as evidenced by falling oil prices that have resulted in lower consumer gasoline prices, the taxes appear to be high enough to avoid the changing incentives that the current U.S. tax provides.

Revenue Effects

With U.S. gasoline consumption generally in the range of 9 million barrels per day (378 million gallons per day), the gasoline tax would have a large base. If, for example, the tax were initially set at $2 per gallon, to achieve a tax inclusive target price of over $5 per gallon, revenues could approach $1 billion per day, minus the effect of conservation.

Revenue on this scale might have a negative effect on the overall purchasing power of the economy, which might be a problem, especially in a recession. This could be ameliorated if tax revenue were recycled back into the economy through increased infrastructure projects, or expenditures on alternative energy projects. If desired, the tax revenue could be returned to households through an income tax rebate program, or a reduction in the income tax rates. If the revenue were returned to taxpayers in this way, the variable gasoline tax could still achieve a portion of its conservation goals through a higher relative price of gasoline, which would discourage consumption.

Revenues generated by the gasoline tax could also assure funding for the Highway Trust Fund, improve the mass transit infrastructure, and fund research and development of alternative energy sources, as well as contribute to deficit reduction.

Refining Industry

The U.S. petroleum refining industry experienced what some have called a "golden age" during the years 2004-2007. A combination of rapidly increasing demand for petroleum products, especially gasoline, coupled with favorable price spreads between high and low quality crude oils, led to high rates of capacity utilization, yielding record profit levels for both the major oil companies and independent refiners. During this period, concern was expressed that U.S. refining capacity was not increasing rapidly enough to keep up with demand growth in the petroleum product markets.

Over the past year, the state of and outlook for the petroleum refining industry have changed. Current weak product demand conditions have resulted in lower capacity utilization rates, refinery closures, and reduced profitability. The near-term outlook suggests continued rationalization will occur in the industry until excess capacity is eliminated.

A key factor in the decline of the refining industry has been reduced gasoline demand, with 2009 consumption about 3.25% less than in 2007. Reduced consumption has resulted from the economic recession, high prices, and inroads in the demand structure made by alternative fuels, mainly ethanol.

A tax on gasoline, to the extent that it reduces gasoline demand, would likely create additional economic pressure on the refining industry. Capacity utilization rates could continue to fall, further plant closures would be likely, and the profit picture could deteriorate even further. If gasoline demand is extremely price inelastic, as discussed in this report, the magnitude of the effects on the refining industry would likely be proportionately small, especially if the gasoline tax was small.

CONCLUSION

The Obama Administration has expressed interest in reduced carbon emissions, reduced dependence on imported oil, and the development of alternative, renewable energy sources. The Highway Trust Fund is in need of an increase in funding. These goals might be attained through an increase in the federal excise tax on gasoline. To facilitate consistent economic decision-making the tax could be set with variable rates, or levels, which would also enhance the predictability of the revenue base.

However, a gasoline tax increase is also likely to be unpopular with consumers. It might also drain purchasing power, especially from an economy that is weakened by recession.

End Notes

[1] Under some cases, economists believe that the price does not rise as much as the tax, but this result depends on supply characteristics, including relative elasticities, that are not likely to apply to petroleum refining.

[2] A more detailed history of the federal excise tax on gasoline can be found in CRS Report RL30304, *The Federal Excise Tax on Gasoline and the Highway Trust Fund: A Short History*, by Pamela J. Jackson, March 29, 2000.

[3] Martin A. Sullivan, Gas Tax Politics, Part I, Taxanalysts Tax History Project, September 22, 2008, available at http://www.taxhistory.org/thp/readings.nsf/ArtWeb/5DDB79194769C2 BF852574 D5003C28D5?OpenDocument.

[4] Ibid.

[5] See CRS Report RL34475, *Transportation Fuel Taxes: Impacts of a Repeal or Moratorium*, by Robert Pirog and John W. Fischer.

[6] Tax revenue may also be used to pay interest on, or retire, national debt, provide a variety of income transfers, or provide aid to foreign nations.

[7] Price elasticity of demand measures the sensitivity of the quantity demanded to variations in price. It is calculated as the percent change in quantity demanded divided by the percent change in price. See James D. Hamilton, *Understanding Crude Oil Prices*, The Energy Journal, Vol. 30, No. 2, pp. 189-192, for price elasticity of oil and gasoline estimates.

[8] Economists use the term social cost to refer to the sum of the private cost of the good plus, or minus, any additional costs accruing to society including, for example, those associated with national security or environmental pollution.

[9] James D. Hamilton, *Understanding Crude Oil Prices*, The Energy Journal, Vol. 30, No.2, 2009, p.180.

[10] Nominal prices are prices not adjusted for inflation.

[11] The U.S. Department of Transportation, Federal Highway Administration estimates that high fuel prices, reduced income growth due to recession, and other factors resulted in a 3.6% decline in road travel in 2008, over 107 billion fewer vehicle miles compared to 2007.

[12] See CRS Report R40053, *Surface Transportation Program Reauthorization Issues for the 111th Congress*, coordinated by John W. Fischer, for more on transit funding issues.

INDEX

D

E

F

G

H

S

T

U

V

W

Y